GOD'S WORD
MADE PLAIN

Written and illustrated
by

MRS. PAUL FRIEDERICHSEN

MOODY PRESS
CHICAGO

Over 200,000 in print

ISBN: 0-8024-3041-4

30

Printed in the United States of America

THE PURPOSE OF THESE LESSONS

This bird's-eye-view course of what the Bible teaches was developed to meet a need. In both foreign and home missionary work in the Philippines and America, I have found that there is a great hunger among churchgoers and nonchurchgoers to know the answers to their spiritual questions. They want a short cut to understand the Bible, and they want to know what they want to know *right now*. This course is designed to give a quick over-all view of the highlights of God's truth, and to whet the appetite for further and deeper study.

There are no new truths in these pages. They are simply the basic teachings of God's Word made plain for both old and young, whether versed in the Bible or not. Understanding these fundamentals of the faith will help in the appreciation of sermons and the better understanding of the Bible. Even the eye-gate has been used to clarify further the important truths of God's Word, and the diagrams and sketches used in this book are those I draw on the blackboard as I teach.

Being so persuaded on the importance of Bible-teaching evangelism, I have used these lessons for the last several years, and rejoiced to see many who have found the answer to their spiritual need through these very studies. An even greater joy was to meet people who have said, "I have never met you before, but my friend brought your lessons over and explained them to me, and now I have received Christ as my Saviour!"

3

When you read or study these pages, please begin at the beginning. Don't skip around and take the last lesson first. Each chapter is based on what has been discussed in the previous chapters, and if they are taken in order, they can be understood more easily.

This bird's-eye-view course is suitable to give to your friends. It has been used to win souls, to establish Christians, and to produce soul-winners.

It is also ideal for use in Bible study classes. Since the material is very brief, looking up other verses with the help of a concordance would provide additional Scripture to discuss for a deeper study. These pages were not intended to be exhaustive studies, but to give the reader a general view of God's will and to arouse a desire to search the Scriptures.

—KAY FRIEDERICHSEN

CONTENTS

1

THE BIBLE

IN THESE DAYS of mushroom-growth religions, many people find their heads spinning with doubts and questions concerning which teaching is right.

"They all claim to be based upon the Bible," argues the confused seeker, "and they seem to have Scripture to back up their theories."

But does *all* Scripture back up *all* they teach? That's the final test. And until we know what God's Word really says we can never know the truth.

It is surprising how many people are willing to take what someone says, or even what they have seen in the movies, or what some church teaches, without searching the Bible for themselves. One mature woman was arguing about the Garden of Eden, and insisting that Eve ate an apple, "I know it was an apple! My Sunday school teacher said so!" A gentleman was arguing with me about some incident in the Bible which he could not prove, and ended his argument by saying, "I know it was so, because I saw it in the movies!"

Error rides on the back of truth. There must be some truth in all wrong teaching, or no one would swallow it. The gullible and untaught in the Word are prone to believe anything that has a Bible verse attached to it. But you can take a verse from the Bible and prove anything you wish. That is where wrong religions begin. Someone gets a brainwave, a bright idea, or has a dream, and then goes to the Bible to find verses to prove it. The prob-

lem is that they take the verse completely out of its context or setting and out of harmony with the rest of the Bible, and thus they can prove just the opposite of what God says! Bible truth is always in harmony with the rest of the Bible. It does not disagree with itself.

Any teaching that is not in harmony with the *whole* Word of God is not God's teaching. No verse should be interpreted apart from its context or the other portion of the Bible. "Knowing this first, that no prophecy of the scripture is of any private interpretation" (II Peter 1:20). This does not mean that a private individual cannot interpret the Bible, but that no portion can be privately interpreted apart from its context. An individual can understand the Bible, even a child—"from a child thou hast known the holy scriptures, which are able to make thee wise unto salvation" (II Tim. 3:15).

In these pages, although I will quote only phrases and isolated verses from God's Word, if you read the context and check the entire Book you will find that we are staying close to the theme and harmony of the entire Book.

The Bible explains itself. When you lack an explanation, then look up other verses on the same subject. Undoubtedly you will find the answer. This is what we are doing in this series of studies. Follow along if you will, and see if we keep our word.

Some people try to select truth by what sounds good to them or what appeals to them intellectually. It usually turns out to be something that pats them on the back and puts a halo on their heads.

"I LIKE THAT CHURCH — IT DOESN'T UPSET MY WAY OF LIVING!"

There is no real common denominator, no standard or basis of judgment other than their own logic. This is not a very dependable gauge, for man's logic is too easily upset by his digestion, the weather, or world conditions, and his discernment varies with his companions or his emotions. In selecting a medicine for an ailment, do we choose something because of its color or taste? Of course not! We examine or go according to the formula. Then why choose a religion by how it appeals to us, or because someone has told us, why not examine the formula?

Throughout olden days God spoke to the human race by means of dreams and visions, angels and voices, and revealed Himself in various forms. "God, who at sundry times and in divers manners spake in time past unto the fathers by the prophets" (Heb. 1:1). Just as we express our thoughts by means of words, so God uses words to communicate with mankind. He uses the voice of nature; the living Word of God, Christ; and the written Word of God, the Bible.

I. God Speaks to Man

A. THE VOICE OF NATURE. Through Nature we see the power of God demonstrated; we see His love in providing for our comfort; we see His glory in the beauty around us; we see His wisdom in the creation of living creatures; we see His infinity in the universe around us. "The heavens declare the glory of God; and the firmament showeth his handiwork. Day unto day uttereth speech, and night unto night showeth knowledge. There is no speech nor language, where their voice is not heard" (Ps. 19:1-3). "For the invisible things of him [God] from the creation of the world are clearly seen, being understood by the things that are made, even his eternal power and Godhead" (Rom. 1:20).

The heavens declare the glory of God

But Nature alone is not the complete revelation of God. It tells nothing of His holiness and judgment, His mercy and salvation, of Heaven and Hell. Nature proves that there is a God, but not His will for us. We need more than the book of Nature.

B. THE LIVING WORD OF GOD. In order that we might know the complete character of God and His will regarding salvation, God Himself came down to dwell among men in the Person of Jesus Christ. Being God, Christ

lived the holiness and mercy of God and spake the judgment and will of God; by His life He gave us an example of Christian living and by His death He provided for our salvation. "In the beginning was the Word, and the Word was with God, and the Word was God. The same was in the beginning with God" (John 1:1, 2). Some try to imply that the Word spoken of here is simply the words of God, His expression and will. But the Word is not just a *thing,* it is a *Person:* "And the Word was made flesh, and dwelt among us" (John 1:14). Christ Himself is the living Word. Revelation 19:11-16 is a description of the coming of Christ to reign after the tribulation. Here He is called the "King of kings, and Lord of lords," and in verse 13, "The Word of God." God "hath in these last days spoken unto us by his Son, whom he hath appointed heir of all things, by whom also he made the worlds. Who being the brightness of his [God's] glory, and the express image of his [God's] person" (Heb. 1:2, 3).

No one can worship God truly in Nature alone, for without the Saviour there is no access to God. Some people say, "I don't need to go to church; I can worship God in Nature. I have as much communion with God out on a picinc or working in my garden or on a hunting trip as in a church." They are probably right too. They have no true communion with God at all! When God has told us expressly how we are to serve Him, and we ignore His commands, then we cannot worship at all. *Worship* means "worth-ship" or "worthy shape," and there is none worthy apart from Christ; we cannot render worth-ship unto God when we are disobedient to God's command to gather together for worship. Disobedience is sin; there is therefore no communion with God!

But Jesus Christ lived here on the earth some 1900 years ago. He is not here today physically, and there had to be some way to preserve His words and will in writing. This record is called God's Word, the *Bible*. The prophets and apostles were led of God to write down the things that God wants us to know and give us a dependable source that is to be our standard for today. By it we test all teachings and dogmas and doctrines just as we gauge all distance by the linear rule.

C. THE WRITTEN WORD OF GOD. The apostle Paul commends the Christians "because, when ye received the word of God which ye heard of us, ye received it not as the word of men, but as it is in truth, the word of God, which effectually worketh also in you that believe" (I Thess. 2:13).

Many people talk about the Bible, but so few actually read it for themselves. Perhaps they glance at it once in awhile or carry it to church and back, or even place it be-

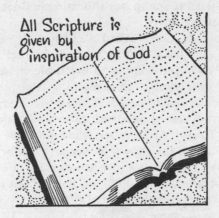

side their bed to gather dust every day, but seldom read it faithfully, consistently and expectantly.

While visiting his parishioners, one minister was trying to impress on them the importance of reading the Bible regularly.

"Oh, pastor," enthused the lady of the house, "I read my Bible every day! However, the last three weeks I could only read one chapter a day instead of the several I used to read because I lost my spectacles."

Before leaving, the minister asked for her Bible to read a portion. There was a hurry and scurry to find the Bible, and eventually one of the boys discovered it on a shelf. The minister took it and it opened automatically to a place where some bulky object kept the pages apart. There were the spectacles! Lost for three weeks in the very Book the lady had said she read every day!

Gossip about the Bible seems to reach everywhere; yet the truth seems locked in the hearts of Christians and seldom gets out. Those who assert that there are mistakes and discrepancies never seem to have seen them for themselves or tried to examine them. For hundreds of years men have tried to stamp out this miracle Book. But it is still the best seller!

Why not give God's Word a chance? It cannot hurt anyone to examine it and let it speak for itself.

One lady stopped coming to my Bible classes because, to use her own words, "That teaching is not the same as I have been raised to believe." Her friend argued with her, "Why not come just for education? You do not have to believe it. Just come to see what the Bible does say." She came back to the classes, and came to know the Word of God, and again in her own words said, "I guess I was raised to believe wrong! I'm glad I found out the truth!"

II. The Origin of the Bible

A. INSPIRATION. "All scripture is given by inspiration of God, and is profitable" (II Tim. 3:16). The actual text of the original manuscripts was literally "God breathed" to godly men, the prophets and apostles, and they wrote what God told them to write even though they didn't fully understand the meaning of all that they wrote. The Bible claims to be the Word of God, and therefore the *only* guide for spiritual truth. It is an accurate history of the good and the bad, the facts and fail-

ings of men, the deeds and words of Satan, the dealings and will of God. God's hand moved His servants as a pen. Just as we might say that our letter was written with a pen, but it is our hand that moved the pen. "For the prophecy came not in old time by the will of man; but holy men of God spake as they were moved by the Holy Ghost" (II Peter 1:21).

To say that the Bible is the Word of God does not mean that every word is His will or His command for us. It is an accurate record of all God wants us to know.

No additions: No subtractions

B. REVELATION. The Bible contains the revelation of God's will and dealings and teachings. The doctrine of salvation, the Christian life, the Church, the second coming of Christ, are all His revelation. These doctrines are those which we plan to take up. There is no new revelation since the writings of the apostles and prophets were completed. A special curse is placed upon any who try to originate new doctrines or manuscripts, or to take away from those already given. "If any man shall add unto these things, God shall add unto him the plagues that are written in this book. And if any man shall take away from the words of the book of this prophecy, God shall take away his part out of the book of life, and out of the holy city" (Rev. 22:18, 19).

But how do we know that the books of the Bible as we have them today are the original books in the Scriptures? True, the original manuscripts have been lost or destroyed. Well, to begin with, at the time of Christ He quoted from the Old Testament books as we have them now. No new books have been added to the Jewish Scriptures and none removed from that time.

Not too long ago some Arab boys were playing in the vicinity of the Dead Sea and discovered some old scrolls embalmed in earthen crocks. When opened up and translated these Dead Sea parchments proved to be Jewish religious writings that were dated long before the birth of Christ. They were quotations from *all* the books of the Old Testament, except Esther, just as we have them today.

But what about the New Testament? In the early church writings in the first centuries A.D., which are still intact, there are quotations from *all* the books of the New Testament as we have them today. So our New Testament was complete at that time. No new books have been added and none subtracted.

All Scripture is not written directly to us. Some of it

regards the nation of Israel, some is pre-Christ and addressed to the Jews. But *all* of it is for us to profit by and to study. "All scripture is given by inspiration of God, and is profitable for doctrine, for reproof, for correction, for instruction in righteousness" (II Tim. 3:16).

C. ILLUMINATION. God does give light upon His Word to those who study it. There is no exhausting the deep meaning and application of this miracle Book. Every time it is read some new truth seems to spring out of the words with new clearness and new encouragement. But illumination of His Word is given by God through the

Holy Spirit. Without the Spirit of God the deep things of God are impossible to be understood. Those who have not received God's way of salvation, the Saviour Jesus Christ, cannot begin to understand the Bible. "Eye hath not seen, nor ear heard, neither have entered into the heart of man, the things which God hath prepared for them that love him. But God hath revealed them unto us by his Spirit. . . . But the natural man receiveth not the things of the Spirit of God: for they are foolishness unto him: neither can he know them, because they are spiritually discerned" (I Cor. 2:9-14).

To read the Bible with an open mind and a sincere prayer for understanding, will bring more light. The excuse is so often given, "I want to know all that the Bible teaches before I make a decision to accept it." No one will ever know *all* that God has written, for His ways are above our ways, and His thoughts are above our thoughts. But we can know enough to see that we are sinners and need a Saviour and that Jesus Christ is the Saviour provided. To act upon this first step will bring more light. When I receive Christ as my personal Saviour, then the Holy Spirit will give me more light. "Light accepted bringeth light; light rejected bringeth night." We take only one step at a time. The more we love our Saviour, the more we will understand of His Word.

Some people are impatient and wonder why they cannot understand everything all at once. Can we expect to know all the council of God at one sitting? Whoever heard of a student comprehending all the books of science and mathematics at one sitting! But they do not throw out their books in disgust the first day of school because they cannot understand all. They enroll in a class and make it their lifework to study, and day after day, line after line, bit by bit, they master their subject. Bible study is a lifework as well as a life pleasure and privilege.

III. The Construction of the Bible

The Book of books is, we may say, a library of sixty-six books bound together in two volumes, the Old Testament and the New Testament. The word *testament* means covenant or agreement or arrangement. It refers to God's means of dealing with the human race from the beginning of time. The Old Testament pertains to things before the coming of Christ. The New Testament deals with God's arrangement for salvation after the coming of Christ.

However, here is something to remember when teaching the Bible. The *death of Christ,* and not His birth, gives us a viewpoint we have not had before. Christ was a Jew; He lived under the Old Testament arrangement and kept the laws for the Jews, and kept the Jewish day of rest. Many of His teachings were to the Jews with the Old Testament approach and application. When Christ died, however, everything was changed. Now we are in the Church Age, under the New Covenant, the New Testament. From Moses to Christ was the age or dispensation of Law; from Pentecost to Christ's return is the Age of Grace, the Church Age.

The Bible is divided into various types of books. The Old Testament is primarily concerned with God's chosen people, the Jews—their history, prophecy, law, and poetry.

The New Testament books, especially from the Gospel of John to Jude, contain Christian doctrine and are especially applicable to us today. Here we find the way of salvation and Christian living. Before Christ's death was the *Old,* since His death is the *New.* The Book of Revelation deals mostly with the future; the Book of Acts is a transition book linking the Old Testament regime with

the New Testament approach, a book of unique experiences and special signs to authenticate the authority of the apostles.

IV. Do All Bibles Have the Same Teaching?

Original manuscripts of the Bible were written in Hebrew and Greek. All Bibles translated honestly from these originals have the same teachings. Both the Roman Catholic and Protestant Bibles were translated from the Hebrew and Greek, so the teachings in both New Testaments are much the same. Any minor difference in wording is due to the method of translation.

The Protestant Bible was translated directly from the original languages into English by some fifty scholars who did not compare renderings until the work was completed. Then the manuscripts were combined to get the best English wording. This is called the King James Version and is still the popular version today.

The Roman Catholic Bible was first translated into Latin by one scholar, Jerome. Later it was translated into English. This two-step process would account for any differences in English. However, the meaning in both Bibles is exactly the same.

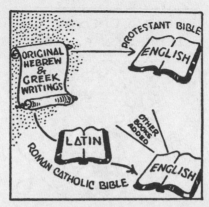

It was at the time of the second translation that the Roman church added the books of the Apocrypha. These books are not included in the Protestant Bible for several reasons: (1) They were added so much later (A.D. 1500) and not included in the Hebrew Scriptures. (2) Neither Christ nor the apostles ever quoted from these books. (3) They are of alien quality and character from the rest of the Bible writings, and Josephus, the Jewish historian, called them "inferior" and unworthy to be included in sacred writ.

They are books of history included in the Old Testament, and have no bearing on Christian doctrine.

V. The Authority of the Bible

Since the Bible is the *only* writing God has given, we must take it *alone* as the basis of religion. If God wanted us to have more information, He would have recorded it for us, and not left it to the imagination of men to fill in the details.

True, John 20:30, 31 says: "And many other signs truly

did Jesus in the presence of his disciples, which are not written in this book: but these are written, that ye might believe that Jesus is the Christ, the Son of God; and that believing ye might have life through his name." Even though there might have been many things that happened in Jesus' time that are not recorded in the Gospels, still we cannot trust traditions or word-of-mouth, to add to God's inspired Word. "All men are liars," and cannot even report accurately a news item that happened the day before; how much less can they be trusted to pass on by word of mouth from century to century the spiritual truths that might mean Heaven or Hell to them that believe?

New dogmas and inventions are constantly appearing in some churches. But if such additions were really from God, then why would He wait for so many centuries to reveal them? The apostle Peter speaks of "vain conversation received by tradition from your fathers" (I Peter 1:18). "Making the word of God of none effect through your tradition, which ye have delivered" (Mark 7:13).

The foundation of our faith is Christ Himself. All the writings of the prophets and apostles are based upon

Him. "Built upon the foundation of the apostles and prophets, Jesus Christ himself being the chief corner stone" (Eph. 2:20). When we build our religion or beliefs on Christ and His teachings alone, we know we are right. Wrong teaching will select parts of the Bible and build upon them their own fabrications and ideas. However, a religion that has even one wrong teaching could not be the truth of God. God does not make even one mistake.

Everyone has a right to his own opinion, but when it comes to a question of truth or error, only the Word of God can be the last authority. "To the law and to the testimony: if they speak not according to this word, it is because there is no light in them" (Isa. 8:20). "If there come any unto you, and bring not this doctrine, receive him not into your house, neither bid him God speed" (II John 10).

One gentleman said to me, "I just can't go along with such teachings about Hell. It's contrary to my upbringing."

"But the Bible teaches more about Hell than it does about Heaven," I said.

"Well, I just can't believe it!" He was fixed in mind.

"Then you mean you do not believe what God says?" I asked.

"Sure, I believe God," he insisted, "but I don't believe in Hell."

"Then someone made a mistake," I said. "If God says there is a Hell, and you say there isn't, then who is right? Either you are wrong or God is wrong!"

VI. The Message of the Bible

The whole Book is a *harmony*. There is but one theme, one Hero, one purpose. Amazing though it may seem, the more than forty different authors who wrote under God's direction have all carried the same message, and their writings dovetail perfectly, even though they lived centuries apart and many did not know what the others had written.

The theme of the Bible is *the Saviour from sin*. God demands the death penalty for sin, for "all have sinned.

. . . There is none righteous, no, not one. . . . All the world is become guilty before God" (Rom. 3). "The wages of sin is death" (Rom. 6:23). "The soul that sinneth, it shall die" (Ezek. 18:4).

Beginning at the Garden of Eden, when Adam and Eve sinned, we see the story of God's atonement portrayed. "Without shedding of blood is no remission" (Heb. 9: 22). God clothed Adam and Eve in the skins of animals. An animal died to provide the skin; blood was shed.

The blood of animals can never take away sin (Heb. 10:11), but it is a picture of the "Lamb of God which taketh away the sin of the world" (John 1:29). Before the world was ever created or mankind was created, Christ was already chosen to be the Substitute to take the death penalty for guilty sinners who would receive Him as their Saviour. All the sacrifices and rituals of the Old Testament were object lessons of the coming Saviour —"the precious blood of Christ . . . a lamb without blemish and without spot" (I Peter 1:19). "Our Lord Jesus Christ . . . gave himself for our sins, that he might deliver us from this present evil world, according to the will of God and our Father" (Gal. 1:3, 4).

A Christian mother told me about her son. He was a flier in World War II. There were three boys in his small bomber that flew over Germany each day, and after working together for so long they had become close friends. One day, coming back after a mission, they were bombarded with heavy anti-aircraft fire that had caught their range and was bursting all around them. The bombardier in the tail of the plane was hit and lay unconscious; then the engine was hit. The pilot endeavored to glide the plane across into the home lines that were so close, and was doing well until another burst of fire tore off one wing. Immediately they went into a tailspin, and the two boys in the cockpit scrambled to jump with their parachutes. Then they remembered their buddy in the back of the plane. As best they could, they grabbed him up, pulled his parachute ripcord, and threw him out. That parachute opened up like a white umbrella and glided slowly in the breeze across the home lines and into safety. The boy was saved.

But there was no time for the other two boys to jump; the whirling plane crashed them to their death.

As that mother stood there telling me the story, with the tears rolling down her face, she smiled proudly, and said, "My boy was the pilot!"

"Greater love hath no man than this, that a man lay down his life for his friends" (John 15.13).

But Jesus Christ died for His enemies. "While we were yet sinners, Christ died for us" (Rom. 5:8).

The coming of Christ brings to life all the details of the Old Testament, for He is the fulfillment of all types and illustrations and the completion of all the law and prophets. He said: "Think not that I am come to destroy the law, or the prophets: I am not come to destroy, but to fulfill" (Matt. 5:17). He came to "fill full," or complete, the *Old* that He might establish the *New*. In the Old Testament men were saved by faith looking for the coming Saviour; in the New Testament we are saved by faith in the Saviour who did come. Salvation is always by faith. We live in the age of grace when we have the New Testament to teach us of the Saviour and His work. We need not to bring the blood of animals to offer on the altar of any temple.

VII. How To Understand the Bible

A. READ AND STUDY IT EVERY DAY. The more we read, the clearer it becomes. "As newborn babes, desire the sincere milk of the word, that ye may grow thereby" (I Peter 2:2). "Search the scriptures; for in them ye think ye have eternal life: and they are they which testify of me" (John 5:39).

B. PRAY AS YOU READ. "Open thou mine eyes, that I may behold wondrous things out of thy law" (Ps. 119:18).

C. LOVE THE AUTHOR. The Bible is God's love-letter to us. When we read it, we learn more of His love and, "we love him because he first loved us." The better we become acquainted with the Lord, the more our hearts warm toward Him, and the more precious His Word becomes.

VIII. How Can We Know that the Bible Is the Word of God?

It's true that the Bible claims to be the Word of God, but are there any proofs outside of the Bible itself? Let's discuss a few things about this miracle Book that certainly do prove its inspiration of God.

A The Bible is a prewritten history, not of just one event, but of many. It gives detailed happenings of the nation of Israel *before they happened;* it tells of the life and death of Christ *before He came;* it tells of the world conditions *before they happen.* Perhaps some will say, "Of course, Jesus fulfilled prophecy; He knew about Scripture and so did what it said." But who made the Roman soldiers cast lots for His vesture and offer Him vinegar and gall? Who told them to nail Him to a cross?

That was a Roman method of execution and not known at the time that David wrote the Psalms that describe crucifixion.

Who made the Roman soldiers pierce His side and not break His legs? Did they know the Scriptures and try to fulfill them?

B. The Bible has a united message, a harmony of teaching, in spite of the fact that there were so many isolated authors over many hundreds of years, and few knew what the others had written. This is beyond mere coincidence.

C. The writers of Scripture very often did not fully understand what they wrote. They could not, because much of what they wrote has only recently come to pass. Consider the incident of Nebuchadnezzar's dream, for instance. Daniel was able to tell him his dream and the interpretation thereof (Dan. 2:37-45). Here Daniel told the king that Babylon was the head of gold in the vision of the great image. That was easy, for Daniel was living in Babylon! But then he prophesied that, "after thee shall arise another kingdom inferior to thee, and another third kingdom of brass, which shall rule over all the earth. And the fourth kingdom shall be strong as iron. . . ." Since Daniel's time the prophecy has come to pass literally.

D. Prophecy already fulfilled and even now coming to pass is solid proof that the other predictions will also be fulfilled. In spite of efforts to discount it, the Bible still holds true.

E. Archaeology and science constantly have to admit that the Bible is right. So-called mistakes of the Bible have turned out to be mistakes of the critics. Back in the time of Moses God commanded those who cared for the sick to "bind a cloth across the mouth," and yet the medical world only gained a knowledge of germs in recent decades. At the time of Columbus people still believed that the earth was flat, and yet thousands of years before, the Bible speaks of "God sitteth upon the circle of the earth."

Men scorned the verse in I Corinthians 15:39: "All flesh is not the same flesh: but there is one kind of flesh of men, another flesh of beasts, another of fishes, and another of birds." Flesh is flesh, they asserted. Blood and bones and flesh are all made up of cells that are common to all species! But within the last hundred years science has had to admit that the cell structure of each species is different from another. That is why there can be no transmutation or mixing of species.

F. Apart from God, how could men have invented the character of a holy God with a heart of love? How could men have conceived a God of all-power who gives to His creatures a free will? How could sinful men have imagined a sinless Christ, or salvation by grace?

G. If the Bible were of human origin, do you think it would have taught the utter depravity of mankind? All false religions are based on the ability of man to improve and save himself by his own efforts and good works.

H. God does not whitewash His heroes. Their sin is mentioned as black as it is. The sins of men and the judgment of God are not "soft-pedaled" as it would be if mere men had written the Bible.

I. According to good editorial procedures, many passages would have been deleted from the Bible if it were man-made. Long lists of names, repetition of rituals, duplications in the Gospels would all have been omitted and smoothed out for easy reading. But God has left them in for some definite purpose, if nothing else than to assure us of His interest and concern in every small detail of our lives.

J. Bible-haters have tried to stamp out the Book down through the ages, but it is still the best seller. "Heaven and earth shall pass away, but my word shall never pass away."

K. Only God's Word can change a down-and-outer into a saint. Philanthropic organizations may try to help fallen man up the ladder of respectability, but none can change his character. They may change his habits, but not his heart.

L. No other book offers a motivating power over sin. There are no end of writings outlining how to be good; no end of platitudes and rules for life, but none can offer any remedy beyond self-improvement for fallen man. But the Word of God offers the Holy Spirit to indwell and enable the believer. The Bible makes living and dying easier!

M. The Bible is a living Book, always up to date, just as practical today as it was 1900 years ago. It satisfies the hungry heart, it guides the confused; it comforts the sorrowing; it enlightens those spiritually blind. The Word of God saves a soul! "Faith cometh by hearing, and hearing by the word of God" (Rom. 10:17).

IX. Why Not Give God's Word a Chance?

Perhaps you have tried many modes of life, many philosophies. Why not give the Bible a chance to prove itself to you? Begin right now. With open mind and searching heart, begin reading it for yourself even as you study these lessons. Look up the verses and read the context and pray as you read, "Lord, I would like to know what Thy Word is all about, and I promise to make an honest effort if Thou wilt help me. Show me what to believe. Amen."

Begin reading the Gospel of John, then read Acts, James, Peter, I John and then any of the New Testament books, and finally read the Old Testament too.

A young mother who did not make a practice of attending church, was indignant when her daughter came home one day, asking, "Mother, do you know God?"

"Of course, I know God! What do you think I am, a heathen?"

"But you do not go to church or read the Bible like my friends' mothers do." The child was insistent.

Partly from hurt pride and partly from self-justification, the mother went to search for a Bible that she once owned. High and low she searched. Eventually she found it at the bottom of a trunk.

But what to read? Shutting her eyes, she opened it at random. It opened at the Book of John. She sat down to read.

Her husband came home for supper. She said to him, "Sit down, and listen to this!" Together they continued to read. It was late when they finished reading the Book of John, and then almost without speaking, they knelt together at the couch and prayed to God to save them.

He did. She is a churchgoing mother today!

QUESTIONS

1. Can the unlearned understand the Bible? (II Tim. 3:15)

2. What does Nature prove to us? (Ps. 19:1-3; Rom. 1:20)

3. Who is the Word? (John 1; 14; Rev. 19:11-16)

4. How did we get our Bible? (II Tim. 3:16; II Peter 1:21)

5. Has God given any new teachings since the Bible was completed? (Rev. 22:18, 19)

6. Who cannot understand the Bible? (I Cor. 2:14)

7. Why was Scripture written? (John 20:31)

8. Can we trust traditions? (I Peter 1:18)

9. What is the foundation of our faith? (Eph. 2:20)

10. How can we discern truth and error? (Isa. 8:20)

11. Should we co-operate with those who do not teach the truth? (II John 10)

12. What is the one main theme of the Bible? (John 1:29; Gal. 1:3, 4)

13. Can the blood of animals take away sin? (Heb. 10:11)

14. What do the Scriptures teach? (John 5:39)

15. What prayer should we pray when we read the Bible? (Ps. 119:18)

16. What brings us to the knowledge of salvation? (II Tim. 3:15)

17. Can we base a teaching on an isolated verse from the Bible? (II Peter 1:20)

18. What is the place of Christ in God's plan? (Heb. 1:2, 3)

19. Were the teachings of the apostles mere words of men? (I Thess. 2:13)

20. What different teachings does the Bible give? (II Tim. 3:16, 17)

2

WHAT IS GOD LIKE?

H OW DO WE KNOW that there is a God?
To those who demand, "Prove to me that there is
a God!" the answer should be, "Prove to us that there is
no God!"

Nature alone is proof enough that there is a God. The
Bible tells us what God is like. "The heavens declare the
glory of God; and the firmament showeth his handiwork.
. . . There is no speech nor language, where their voice
is not heard" (Ps. 19:1, 3) . "Because that which may be
known of God is manifest in them [who doubt there is a
God]; for God hath showed it unto them. For the invisible things of him [God] from the creation of the world
are clearly seen, being understood by the things that are
made, even his eternal power and Godhead; so that they
are without excuse" (Rom. 1:19, 20)

I. Who Is God?

"God is a Spirit: and they that worship him must worship him in spirit and in truth" (John 4:24) .

A spirit is a person; a person is a spirit. God is not
merely influence or mind or subconsciousness—He is a
living Person having knowledge, feeling, will, righteousness, love, and all the qualifications that distinguish persons from the animal world.

There are different kinds of spirits or persons—God-
persons; angel-persons which include good and bad angels, Satan and demons; human-persons. All are im-

MOSES AND THE BURNING BUSH

mortal and will live throughout eternity. However, only human beings are limited to physical bodies while here on the earth. God has revealed Himself to men in various physical forms. He appeared to Moses in the burning bush; to Job in the whirlwind; to Adam and Eve in the cool of the evening, but it was not until the Son of God "became flesh and dwelt among us" (John 1:14) that God took human form and lived here on the earth. Mary is not the "mother of God," for God has no beginning, but she conceived the body in which God would dwell. Satan and angels too have appeared in visible forms throughout Bible history, but spirits or persons are invisible reality.

II. God Is a Triune God

The word *trinity* is not used in Scripture, but the meaning of "three-in-one" is very evidently set forth. Beginning with the very first verse in the Bible, the Hebrew language says: "In the beginning God [Elohim, a three-person word] created [a singular word] the heaven [a two-number word; two heavens were created, the third heaven is eternal] and the earth [singular]" (Gen. 1:1).

Then in verse 26, God said, "Let *us* make man in *our* image." Did God refer to the angels with that plural word? No. The next verse answers that. "So God created man in his own image."

The Bible teaches that God the Father is God (Rom. 1:7).

God the Son is called God (Col. 2:9; Heb. 1:8).

God the Holy Spirit is called God (Acts 5:3, 4).

All are equal in glory, in power, and in characteristics. All three Persons have the unique attributes of God. The name of God is never coupled with men or other persons as it is in the benediction found in II Corinthians 13:14. "The grace of the Lord Jesus Christ, and the love of God, and the communion of the Holy Ghost, be with you all. Amen." It could never be said the grace of the Lord Jesus Christ and the love of Mr. Jones or the fellowship of Sister Brown.

Consider the great commission in Matthew 28:19, 20: "Go ye therefore, and teach all nations, baptizing them in the name of the Father, and of the Son, and of the Holy Ghost." How inappropo it would be to say, "In the

name of the Father and of the Son and of Pastor Smith"!
God's name is coupled only with God.

At the baptism of Jesus, we find the Trinity represented all at the same time. Jesus was being baptized, the Holy Spirit descended in the form of a dove, and the Father spoke from Heaven. Jesus Himself says in John 14:16, 17: "*I* will pray the *Father,* and he shall give you another Comforter . . . the *Spirit of truth.*"

Then what is meant by Christ being called the "Son of God"? Does this mean that Christ is created by God the Father? Christ is the *eternal Son.* Being the Son of God refers to His *relationship* and not to His origin. Christ

was never created by God the Father, for He is Himself God. Look up these verses that actually call Christ God: I Timothy 3:15; John 1:1-3, 14; Romans 9:5; I John 5:20; I Timothy 3:16; Matthew 1:23.

Christ was physically "begotten by the Father" when He was born a human being, and He is also called the "first begotten from the dead" when He rose from the grave (Col. 1:18). The Jehovah of the Old Testament is the Lord in the New Testament, and both refer to the Lord God and the Lord Jesus Christ (Acts 2:32-36).

God is one in essence and one in Godhead, but *three in Person*. "The Lord our God is *one* Lord" (Deut. 6:4). Then how can He be three in Person? The Hebrew word used here *one* is again a plural word. It has the same meaning as when God says husband and wife shall be one flesh. It has a compound unity just as we speak of one family (which is made up of several members) or one herd of cattle, or one crowd.

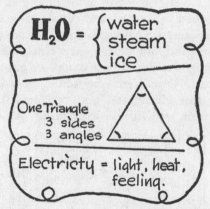

$$H_2O = \begin{cases} \text{water} \\ \text{steam} \\ \text{ice} \end{cases}$$

One Triangle
3 sides
3 angles

Electricty = light, heat, feeling.

Nature has many trinities. Man is made up of body, soul, and spirit. Electricity has light, feeling, and heat. An equilateral triangle has three equal angles and three equal sides. But none of these correctly illustrate the Trinity because God the Father is not a *part* of God, or the Son or the Holy Spirit a part of God. Each is fully God.

Perhaps we could use the illustration of the chemical formula H_2O. When two parts hydrogen and one part oxygen are liquid, they are called water. When they are hot, they produce steam; when they are cold, they are ice. All three forms are the same chemical formula, but are manifested in different forms. God is one in essence but three in Person.

Once again, let us illustrate as we speak of *mankind*. Suppose there were only three persons in the human race, all three would be mankind, but three persons. Now if it were possible to take liberty in coining a new word, let us contrast mankind with *God-kind*. There is only one God-kind, but three Persons. All three are God, but each has His own office and work.

You say you cannot understand this truth about the triune God? Well, there are a lot of things we cannot understand even in Nature, and yet we carry on and believe them because we have seen that they are a fact. We cannot understand how we can eat a chicken dinner that gives us strength to do our work, but we eat our dinner just the same! As so often questioned, how is it that a brown cow eats green grass and produces white milk? So from now on we will not drink milk! We cannot un-

derstand how it came about! Well, if there are so many things in Nature that we cannot understand and yet we take them by faith and enjoy them, then why should we object when there are things God says which we cannot understand? After all, He made the cow; should we not expect that He has other truths that are also higher than our finite minds can grasp? "For my thoughts are not your thoughts, neither are your ways my ways, saith the Lord. For as the heavens are higher than the earth, so are my ways higher than your ways, and my thoughts than your thoughts" (Isa. 55: 8, 9).

From the following diagram we see the work of each member of the Godhead.

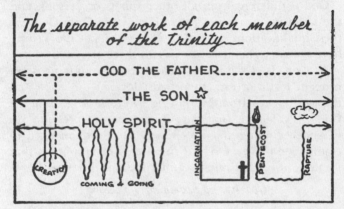

God the Father is always spoken of as in Heaven. He took part in creation, and His glory was manifested in the tabernacle and temple.

God the Son took part in creation; He appeared to men in human form as "the angel of the Lord" during Old Testament times, but became flesh and was born of a virgin when He came to earth to dwell for thirty-three years. After His death and resurrection, He returned to glory where He is now at the right hand of the throne of God, and will some day come back to earth again.

God the Holy Spirit took part in creation. During the Old Testament days He came upon men to bless and help but did not remain with them forever. The Holy Spirit came upon Mary when she conceived the body in which Christ would dwell. He came upon Christ at His baptism and during His ministry. He took part in the resurrection of Christ. On the day of Pentecost the Holy Spirit came to dwell on the earth to convict and convert sinners. He is here today and will remain here until the Church is taken to Heaven.

III. The Characteristics of God

God is different from all other spirits or persons, and the following attributes prove His deity. Only God has these qualifications, and all three members of the Trinity have the same characteristics, so all three are *God*.

A. GOD IS ETERNAL. "Before the mountains were brought forth, or ever thou hadst formed the earth and the world, even from everlasting to everlasting, thou art God" (Ps. 90:2). God lives in the eternal present. He has no beginning and no ending. He does not need to count time by years. He is *infinite*. The trouble is that we are *finite*. Our minds cannot fathom the meaning of

God has no beginning, no ending

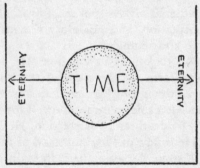

eternity! Our concept of time is limited to the past history of mankind, a bare four-to-six thousand years at the most. Because we cannot understand infinity, does that mean that there is no such thing? Eternity and infinity are both beyond our ken. "One day is with the Lord as a

thousand years, and a thousand years as one day"
(II Peter 3:8). This does not necessarily mean that when
the Bible speaks of one day it means always a thousand
years! The Bible was written for men, and much of its
measure of time is human measurement. Unless it is explained to mean something else, time measurements in
the Bible are literal years as we know them.

God is self-existent. Here again we cannot understand
how this can be. How could anyone have no beginning?
How could anyone always be and give himself life? "Anyone" could not! God is not "anyone," He is GOD almighty! "The Father hath life in himself" (John 5:26).
God is the "I AM," the eternal, self-existent One. "And
God said unto Moses, I AM THAT I AM" (Exod. 3:14).

Christ is not only called God, but has this attribute of
God: He is eternal (John 17:5; Isa. 9:6; Heb. 13:8; Col.
1:17).

The Holy Spirit is eternal (Heb. 9:14).

B. GOD IS THE CREATOR. "In the beginning God created the heaven and the earth" (Gen. 1:1). To "create"
means to make something out of nothing. Beginning with
nothing, God brought into being the universe by the
word of His mouth. When God said, "Let there be,"
things came into being. How hard science has tried to
refute this truth of the Bible! How they have worked at
proving another origin of things besides God! And in
every case they have to come back to the beginning and
admit "We don't know." Since the Word of God has
proved itself in so many other ways, and since prophecy
and archaeology and science all prove that God's Word
is true, why not take God's Word about creation?

But notice Christ's part in creation: "For by him were
all things created, that are in heaven, and that are in
earth, visible and invisible, whether they be thrones, or
dominions, or principalities, or powers: all things were

created by him, and for [through] him: and he is [notice the present tense for Christ too, is the I AM, Jehovah] before all things, and by him all things consist [hold together]" (Col. 1:16-18) .

Then again: "The same was in the beginning with God. All things were made by him: and without him was not anything made that was made" (John 1:2, 3) .

The Holy Spirit, too, takes part in creation. "And the Spirit of God moved upon the face of the waters" (Gen. 1:2) .

Atheists who defy God and reject Jesus Christ are actually "held together" by the very One they defy! How ironical! Just as a paper doll might turn on the one who cut it out and say, "I don't believe you exist!"

C. GOD IS ALL-POWERFUL (OMNIPOTENT) . "Then Job answered the Lord, and said, I know that thou canst do everything" (Job 42:1, 2) . There is nothing that God cannot do, but there are two things God *will not* do—He will not sin, and He *will not force the will of men.* God has given us a free will to choose to love and obey Him, and He leaves the choice with us.

When we speak of the will of God, do not forget that

there are two phases. There is the primary or perfect will of God, that which He desires and for which He made man—"that we might love and glorify him and enjoy him forever." God is "not willing that any should perish, but that all should come to repentance" (II Peter 3:9).

On the other hand, we have the permissive will of God. Because men choose to resist God's will and seek their own ways instead, they find that "there is a way which seemeth right unto a man, but the end thereof are the ways of death" (Prov. 14:12). There are many passages of pathos in the Bible, but some of the most moving are the words of Christ: "Ye will not come to me, that ye might have life" (John 5:40). "How often would I have gathered thy children together, even as a hen gathereth her chickens under her wings, and ye would not!" (Matt. 23:37).

The amazing fact is: the God who can do anything and everything, who created us, *will not force our will!* He gives us a free choice. Here again is proof of the truth of the Bible! No human mind could imagine a God like that!

Yes, God is all-powerful; and yet we limit the power

of God by our own unbelief, by our prayerlessness and by
our sinfulness!

On the other hand, what a joy to know that we have
a God "that is able to do exceeding abundantly above
all that we ask or think, according to the power that
worketh in us" (Eph. 3:20).

Jesus Christ is all-powerful (Matt. 28:18).

The Holy Spirit is the Spirit of power (Luke 1:35).

D. GOD IS UNCHANGEABLE (IMMUTABLE). "For I am
the Lord, I change not" (Mal. 3:6). "The Father of
lights, with whom is no variableness, neither shadow of
turning" (James 1:17). God's attitude is always the same
toward righteousness and sin. He never changes His
mind, for He knows the end from the beginning. Someone will ask, "Then why did God change His word in regard to Nineveh? No wonder Jonah did not want to
preach to that town when he knew God might not bring
the judgment upon it that Jonah was supposed to pre-
dict!" But do not forget that God changed the judgment
upon Nineveh because Nineveh changed its ways. God
changed His dealings with those people as they changed
their ways. God will always punish sin; when men repent and change their ways, God can bless instead of
punish.

Christ is unchangeable (Heb. 13:8).

The Holy Spirit is unchangeable (John 14:16).

E. GOD IS EVERYWHERE (OMNIPRESENT). "Whither
shall I go from thy spirit? Or whither shall I flee from
thy presence? If I ascend up into heaven, thou art there.
. . . If I take the wings of the morning, and dwell in the
uttermost parts of the sea; even there shall thy hand lead
me, and they right hand shall hold me" (Ps. 139:7-10).

God is in all parts of the universe and near each person.
In His creation-power God keeps the world running, the
vegetation growing, animal life and human life continu-

ing. God is everywhere in His power to hold things together. Can it be said that God is on a desert island where there are no people? If He were not there in His creation-power, how would the grass grow or the island hold together? He is everywhere to hold things together, to keep the grass growing, the insects alive, and the sea within its bounds.

However, when a man is on that island, then it can be said that God is there in a special sense to do His office work in the heart of that human being.

"Am I a God at hand, saith the Lord, and not a God afar off? Can any hide himself in secret places that I shall not see him? saith the Lord. Do not I fill heaven and earth? saith the Lord" (Jer. 23:23, 24). We cannot hide from God.

Jesus Christ is omnipresent (Matt. 28:20).

The Holy Spirit is omnipresent (Ps. 139:7-10).

F. GOD IS ALL-KNOWING (OMNISCIENT). "O Lord, thou hast searched me, and known me. Thou knowest my downsitting and mine uprising, thou understandest my thought afar off. Thou compassest my path and my lying down, and art acquainted with all my ways. For there is not a word in my tongue, but, lo, O Lord, thou knowest it altogether. Thou hast beset me behind and before, and laid thine hand upon me. Such knowledge is too wonderful for me; it is high, I cannot attain unto it" (Ps. 139:1-6).

For those who love Him, this is such a comfort to know that God knows the past, the present, and the future, and all things are in His hands! He knows our name and

address and telephone number! He knows how many hairs on our head! "But the very hairs of your head are all numbered" (Matt. 10:30). "Wherefore, if God so clothe the grass of the field, which today is, and tomorrow is cast into the oven, shall he not much more clothe you, O ye of little faith?" (Matt. 6:30). The marvel of it all is this: here is an almighty God who made all things and can do all things, and yet He cares enough to keep track of our every need and heartbreak. Does God care when we are sick or troubled or bereaved? Indeed He does! If we have received Christ as our personal Saviour, He cares and knows and is alongside to help. "He knows, He loves, He cares!"

For those who neglect God, this truth is a terrifying

one. To know that God knows every thought and deed, and we cannot hide from Him, is enough to make every sinner tremble. Excuses do not stand up before an all-knowing God. If people were a little more conscious of this attribute of God they would be a little less glib in excuses to stay away from church and from prayer meeting!

Christ is also all-knowing (John 2:24).

The Holy Spirit is all-knowing (I Cor. 2:10, 11).

G. GOD IS HOLY. "Exalt ye the Lord our God, and worship at his footstool; for he is holy" (Ps. 99:5).

It must be because people do not fully appreciate this truth of God's holiness that there is so much carelessness and such a shallow idea of God, and yet the truth of God's holiness is paramount throughout the whole Bible. There seems to be a growing indifference to sin even among Christians today, and people think that just because God is a God of love that He does not know the difference between right and wrong. How far from true! It takes a full realization of God's holiness to convict us of our sin. *Holy* means "without sin." "God is light, and in him is no darkness at all" (I John 1:5). Darkness represents sin and ignorance, and light stands for righteousness and truth. All truth originates with God and is recorded in His Word. There is no spiritual insight apart from the Bible. Truth is always connected with personality. God is a Person, and all truth and righteousness are in Him.

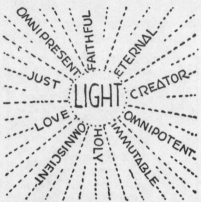

But God is not only holy Himself, He demands that no sin enter His presence, so Heaven must be holy. Not one sin can enter His Holy City. "And there shall in no wise enter into it anything that defileth, neither whatsoever worketh abomination, or maketh a lie: but they which are written in the Lamb's book of life" (Rev. 21:27). Note how the sin of lying is included right along with the abomination of defilement! Even one lie is enough to exclude one from the holy presence of God.

Satan was cast out of Heaven when sin was found in his heart, and every unforgiven sinner must be barred from the presence of the Holy God. "All that do unrighteously are an abomination unto the Lord thy God" (Deut. 25:16). When Christ hung on the cross as the Sin-bearer for man's sin, God the Father had to hide His face from His own Son. Christ cried, "My God, my God, why hast thou forsaken me?"

How then can guilty sinners ever hope to stand before the holy God? They cannot. They need a Saviour!

Christ is holy (I Peter 2:22).

The Holy Spirit is holy (Rom. 1:4).

H. GOD IS THE RIGHTEOUS JUDGE. "The Lord is in his holy temple, the Lord's throne is in heaven: his eyes behold, his eyelids try, the children of men. The Lord trieth the righteous: but the wicked and him that loveth violence his soul hateth. Upon the wicked he shall rain snares, fire and brimstone, and a horrible tempest: this shall be the portion of their cup" (Ps. 11:4-6).

God must always judge sin. His justice is not blind; His holiness demands the death penalty. Because God knows all things, His judgment is righteous. "Shall not the Judge of all the earth do right?" (Gen. 18:25). But God can never overlook sin.

Christ will actually be the Judge some day (John 5:22). Because He died for man's sins, He will be the One to judge those who reject His salvation.

What a terrible thing it would be if this lesson ended with this theme! But it does not.

I. GOD IS LOVE. "But God commendeth his love toward us, in that, while we were yet sinners, Christ died for us" (Rom. 5:8).

Although God's holiness cuts man from the presence of God, and although His justice demands the death

penalty, yet God's love has provided a way of salvation to take sin away. That "way" is a Person, God Himself— "Christ died for our sins." God hates sin, but He loves the souls of sinners. The love of God is poured out upon a guilty world by the blood of Jesus Christ that was shed on Calvary for our sin. His atonement is sufficient for the whole world, but *efficient* only to those who receive Him as their personal Saviour. "For the Son of man is come to seek and to save that which was lost" (Luke 19: 10).

Note this, however: the salvation provided and offered by Christ's death is only to those who receive Him. Every promise of salvation is hinged on the words, "he that believeth" (receiveth). Our part is to receive the Saviour, and God is the One to save from sin and Hell. Just analyze the most well-known verse in the Bible—John 3:16. There are five parts to the verse. Let us see which parts are ours and which are God's.

GOD'S PART	OUR PART

For God so loved the world......

that he gave his only begotten Son

.... that whosoever believeth in him
[receives Christ as personal
Saviour]

should not perish...............

but have everlasting life.........

Four parts are God's work, and only one part is ours.
But although God has already done His part and loved
us and provided a Saviour for us, He cannot take His
next part to keep us from Hell and give us eternal life
until we do our part. Our only part is to *receive Him*.
Just as in a game of checkers—God cannot take a second
turn until we take our turn. So our free will holds back
the power of God to save. If we are lost, it is because we
reject God's way of salvation.

So many people think, "God is a God of love, He could
never send anyone to Hell!" Yes, God is a God of love,
but He is also a God of holiness and justice. Those who
neglect His way of salvation and trample under foot the
Son of God deserve eternal separation from God.

God has placed stop signs on the road to Hell. The

GOD'S STOPSIGNS   HELL

first warning is His Word. Those who pass up the Word of God are passing up God's warning of sin and Hell. Then too, God has placed Christians as stop signs to warn men to flee from the wrath to come. The trouble is that these stop signs are not always in working order! If our Christian life is not consistent, we may be the cause of someone passing on into eternity without God and without hope.

While driving through the countryside one night, we passed up a side road where I knew there was a stop sign. I mentioned it to my husband who was driving, but he said, "I saw no sign there." "But there is one there," I said, "I've seen it many times." We backed up to see. The sign was there all right, but a heavy snow had covered the face of the sign so that it did not reflect the light! There but not working! We might have had an accident.

Some Christians are like that sign—not in working condition! We are responsible for more than seeing that we get to Heaven ourselves, we are responsible to be a witness to others.

The other stop sign that God has placed on life's road is His own Son. Those who pass up the Word of God, reject the witness of the saints of God, and neglect the Son of God deserve everlasting Hell. "If we sin willfully [that is, we reject the Saviour and trample under foot His blood] after that we have received the knowledge of the truth [we have known the way of salvation], there remaineth no more sacrifice for sins [there is no other Saviour], but a certain fearful looking for of judgment and fiery indignation" (Heb. 10:26, 27). There is no excuse for anyone going to Hell.

J. GOD IS FAITHFUL AND TRUE. "If we confess our sins, he is faithful and just to forgive us our sins, and to cleanse us from all unrighteousness" (I John 1:9). "He

abideth faithful: he cannot deny himself" (II Tim. 2:13).
God will keep His word. He cannot lie.

Our salvation does not depend upon our feelings or
our works, but upon the faithful keeping power of God.
He promises eternal life to those who receive Him, and
He cannot lie. We have eternal life and shall *never
perish;* that is His promise. We take Him as our Saviour,
and then He takes us to Heaven. Our part is to receive
Him; His part is to save us.

Often seeking souls have said to me, "I wanted to be
saved, and I prayed to God to save me, but I've felt nothing since. I guess nothing happened!"

"Just what did you expect to feel?" I usually ask.

"Well," they usually say, "a friend of mine was literally
walking on air when he was saved. He kept talking
about joy and a wonderful feeling. I have not had any
such feeling."

It is a simple matter to help honest seekers, and to show
them that we are saved by receiving the Saviour and not
by how we feel afterward. Everyone is made differently.
Some shout and yell at a ball game and some sit quietly;

both enjoy the game! They have different natures, that is all. Too many people are seeking some feeling or emotional upheaval as a sign of their salvation. The real sign of salvation is a desire to please God and hate sin.

Not long ago a lady said, "When I asked Christ to save me, nothing happened!"

"How do you know nothing happened?" I asked.

"Well, I didn't feel anything."

As I went through the steps of salvation with her, I asked her each time, "Do you believe that you are a sinner?" She said, "Yes." "Do you believe Christ alone is the Saviour?" "Yes." "Do you believe God's way of salvation is to receive Him?" "Yes." "Do you want to be saved and live for God?" "Yes, I do."

"Then," I said, "forget the past lack of feeling. Will you receive Christ right now, and settle it once for all?"

"Yes, I will." She seemed sincere.

We prayed together, and then I asked her, "Did you ask Christ to save you?"

"Yes, I did."

"Will He lie to you?"

"No, I do not believe He will."

"Now look what He says here in John 3:16: 'That whosoever believeth in him should not perish.' Is that a promise?"

"Yes."

"Did you believe Him and ask Him to save you?"

"Yes."

"Then what does He say?"

"I have eternal life and shall never perish."

"Do you believe God?"

"Oh, yes, I do! I feel better already!"

"Well, do not count on feeling anything. Tomorrow you may have indigestion and feel bad! Count on God's keeping His word. He cannot lie. Feelings of joy will follow."

"Faithful is he that calleth you, who also will do it" (I Thess. 5:24). "And being fully persuaded that, what he had promised, he was able also to perform" (Rom. 4:21). Yes, joy and peace and assurance do come to fill the life of a Christian, but that is not our *proof* of salvation; our proof is *God will keep His word*. We are saved by faith in a faithful God.

QUESTIONS

1. How can we know there is a God? (Rom. 1:19, 20)
2. How should we worship God? (John 4:24)
3. How do we know that God is three Persons? (Matt. 3:16, 17; 28:19; John 14:16; II Cor. 13:14)
4. How do we know Christ is God? (Heb. 1:8)
5. When did God begin? (Ps. 90:2)
6. Is Christ the Creator? (Col. 1:16-18)
7. What will God not do? (John 5:40)
8. Is God in Hell? (Ps. 139:7-10) (This is fully answered in the lesson on Souls After Death.)

9. Does God know our needs and problems? (Matt. 6:30)

10. Who may not enter the Holy City? (Rev. 21:27)

11. Who will be the Judge? (John 5:22)

12. How does God advertise His love to us? (Rom. 5:8)

13. How can we know we are saved? (John 3:16) ⌐

14. When was Christ "begotten from the dead"? (Col. 1:18)

15. Why can't we fully understand infinity, eternity, the Trinity, etc.? (Isa. 55:8, 9)

16. Who holds the world together? (Col. 1:17)

17. Does Christ know everything? (John 2:24)

18. Can God tolerate a little sin? (Deut. 25:16)

19. What is God's way of salvation? (John 3:16) What is our part?

20. Do our feelings prove we are saved? (I John 1:9)

3

THE HOLY SPIRIT

THE HOLY SPIRIT IS GOD (Acts 5:3, 4). The third member of the Trinity, the Holy Spirit is equal in glory and power and honor with God the Father and God the Son, and is called the Spirit of God and the Spirit of Christ.

Some believe that the Holy Spirit is an influence or power. He is a *Person*, not an *it*. There is no influence without personality, and the Spirit of God has influence. He also has knowledge, feeling, will, love, and every qualification attributed to personality. He is called the eternal Spirit and has all the attributes of God.

In creation "the Spirit of God moved upon the face of the waters" (Gen. 1:2). He is the Creator.

Throughout the days before Christ's coming, which we call the Old Testament days, the work of the Holy Spirit

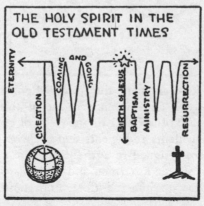

THE HOLY SPIRIT IN THE OLD TESTAMENT TIMES

was to come upon men to help and bless them as long as they were obedient to God, but He left them when they sinned. He did not abide in their hearts forever. He came upon King Saul to bless him as long as he obeyed God, but when Saul sinned, an evil spirit came upon him. When King David sinned, he prayed, "Take not thy holy Spirit from me" (Ps. 51:11).

It was the Holy Spirit who came upon the virgin Mary so that she conceived the body in which Christ would dwell; He came upon Christ at His baptism; He worked in Christ during His earthly ministry; He took part in the resurrection of Christ. But it was not until the day of Pentecost that the Spirit of God came to make His abode in the earth and to dwell forever in the hearts of believers.

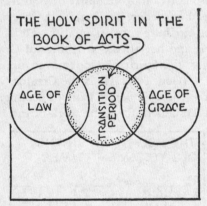

Consider for a moment the unique Book of the Acts of the Apostles. This is an account of the transition between the age of law and the new age of grace. There were many incidents and events that occurred in this period that were designed to authenticate the authority of the group of simple fishermen and uneducated followers of Christ. Try to imagine these unprepossessing men whose Leader, Jesus, had been killed. There was only their word to prove that Jesus had risen from the dead; only their word to prove that He had ascended to Heaven. Now just who was going to believe them?

In His graciousness, God bestowed upon them the gifts of miracles and signs, and upon them came the power of the Holy Spirit on the day of Pentecost. The skeptical Jews and unbelieving Gentiles could not gainsay the miracles and wonders, neither could they resist the powerful preaching on the day of Pentecost, and thousands turned to God. But do not forget that these signs and miracles were given to the early church period for this special purpose. They had no New Testament. They had nothing but the word of the apostles. "How shall we escape, if we neglect so great salvation; *which at the first* began to be spoken by the Lord, and was confirmed unto us by them that heard him; God also bearing them witness, both with signs and wonders, and with divers miracles, and gifts of the Holy Ghost" (Heb. 2:3, 4). Notice it says these signs were given "at the first."

Today, however, we do have the written Word of the New Testament. Just as the birth of Christ was a one-time event that is never to be repeated, so the birth of the Church, the day of Pentecost, is a one-time event that need not be repeated.

In the age, or dispensation, of law, the emphasis was upon physical blessings and miracles. Christ lived in that dispensation, and His greatest work was physical miracles to prove His deity. He said to His disciples: "Greater works than these shall he do; because I go unto my Father. And whatsoever ye shall ask in my name, that will I do, that the Father may be glorified in the Son" (John 14:12, 13).

But what greater miracles could men do than raise the dead, still the stormy sea, and turn water into wine?

Yes, there is one greater miracle! And that is the salvation of souls! It was this miracle that we see especially in the ministry of the apostle Paul, also of Peter on Pentecost and of the other apostles and evangelists throughout history, and this is the predominating work of the Holy Spirit in the world today. Just what does Christ say about the work of the Spirit of God?

I. The Holy Spirit Teaches about the Saviour

Jesus said: "But the Comforter [the one who goes alongside to help], which is the Holy Ghost, whom the Father will send in my name, he shall teach you all things, and bring all things to your remembrance, whatsoever I have said unto you" (John 14:26). "But when the Comforter is come, whom I will send unto you from the Father, even the Spirit of truth, which proceedeth from the Father, he shall testify of me" (John 15:26). "Howbeit when he, the Spirit of truth, is come, he will guide you into all truth: for he shall not speak of himself; but whatsoever he shall hear, that shall he speak: and will show you things to come. He shall glorify me" (John 16:13, 14).

The Spirit of God does not emphasize Himself. He always points to Christ. He is honored when Christ is upheld. After all, it was Christ who died for our sins and it is the work of the Spirit to teach men about the Saviour. He does this by making clear the teachings God has given in His Word. Without the help of the Holy Spirit man cannot comprehend God's will.

An intellectual man said to me, "Why is it that apparently uneducated, simple people, who call themselves Christians, seem to understand the Bible better than some university men with degrees?"

I suggested that we read some verses from I Corinthians. If you want the answer to this question, please read the following references: I Corinthians 1:18-27; 2:5-14; Romans 1:19-22.

After reading the Bible passages, the gentleman said, "I see I need God on my side to help me understand the Bible."

"Yes," I replied, "and there is no better time to investigate these things than right now. Would you be willing to attend one of my Bible classes and search out these things?"

He agreed. He did come and kept coming, and found Christ as his own Saviour; today he wonders why he ever asked such a question!

II. The Holy Spirit Convicts Men of Sin

Jesus said: "And when he [the Holy Spirit] is come, he will reprove the world of sin . . . of sin, because they believe not on me" (John 16:8, 9).

The sin of unbelief—of not receiving the Saviour—is the sin that sends sinners to Hell. The Spirit of God convicts men of sin by speaking to their consciences through the Word of God and the testimony of believers.

Sometimes people resent preachers that speak the truth

too plainly! They often take offense when confronted with Bible truths! They find a church that will not make them uncomfortable, and a preacher who will soothe their ruffled consciences with comforting words. Little do they realize that they are actually resisting the convicting power of the Holy Spirit Himself.

Jesus Christ said, "Behold I stand at the door and knock" (Rev. 3:20). Since Christ is in Heaven bodily today, it is the Spirit of Christ, the Holy Spirit who does the knocking on the heart of the sinner.

Unless we realize our sin and open our life to the Saviour, we resist the work of the Spirit. "Ye do always resist the Holy Ghost: as your fathers did, so do ye" (Acts 7:51).

III. The Holy Spirit Converts Sinners into Saints of God

Jesus said: "And when he is come, he will reprove the world of sin, and of righteousness . . . of righteousness, because I go to my Father, and ye see me no more" (John 16:8, 10).

Conversion means a change of mind that results in a

change of action; it is an "about face" from sin to right-eousness, from Hell to Heaven, from Satan unto God. When we respond to the convicting voice of God and receive Christ as our personal Saviour, we begin a new life; we are converted; saved. The converted life is a righteous life. Because Christ has finished His work of salvation and has returned to glory and ever lives to intercede for us, His righteousness is now available for

GLAMORIZING DOESN'T CHANGE SINNERS INTO SAINTS

SATAN

REFORM

LOST SINNER

us who receive Him. "Wherefore he is able also to save them to the uttermost that come unto God by him, see-ing he ever liveth to make intercession for them" (Heb. 7:25).

"Baptized" into God and "baptism of the Holy Ghost" both refer to the act of becoming *one in Christ*, by re-ceiving the Saviour. "Christ in you, the hope of glory" (Col. 1:27). "For by one Spirit are we all baptized into one body [Christ] . . . and have been all made to drink into one Spirit" (I Cor. 12:13). This is not referring to water baptism or to some emotional second experience in the Christian life, but to *salvation*. We are immersed into Christ, and He is in us. It is a union of faith and love that nothing can break asunder.

"IMMERSED" INTO CHRIST—

Baptism into Christ begins for us a new life of right-eousness. "Therefore if any man be in Christ, he is a new creature [creation]: old things are passed away; behold, all things are become new. And all things are of God" (II Cor. 5:17, 18). We do not need to agonize and pray for this baptism. Christ waits to come in if we only open the door.

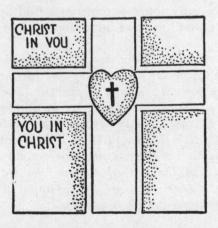

CHRIST IN YOU

YOU IN CHRIST

IV. The Holy Spirit Indwells the Believer

Jesus said: "And I will pray the Father, and he shall give you another Comforter, that he may abide with you forever; even the Spirit of truth" (John 14:16, 17). The Holy Spirit never leaves those who have received Him. "Know ye not that ye are the temple of God, and that the Spirit of God dwelleth in you?" (I Cor. 3:16). "What? Know ye not that your body is the temple of the Holy Ghost which is in you, which ye have of God, and ye are not your own?" (I Cor. 6:19).

The Holy Spirit indwells believers

It is a serious thing to remember that we are indwelt by the Holy Spirit. Our life must be holy. But we cannot be holy by ourselves; only the indwelling Christ can give us victory over sin and the Devil "And when he [the Spirit] is come, he will reprove the world of . . . judgment, because the prince of this world is judged" (John 16:8, 11). Victory is available. Satan is a potentially defeated foe! "But thanks be to God, which giveth us the victory through our Lord Jesus Christ" (I Cor. 15:57).

The Spirit of God never leaves the believer—"that he may abide with you *forever*." "I will never leave thee, nor forsake thee" (Heb. 13:5). He does not stay outside the tavern while a Christian takes a drink; He does not wait outside the dance hall while a Christian spends his evening in the arms of godless companions, the Holy Spirit is in us and will be with us forever. We drag His name in the dust when we sin. This alone is reason enough why a Christian should be holy.

V. The Holy Spirit Seals the Believer

"The holy Spirit of God, whereby ye are sealed unto the day of redemption" (Eph. 4:30). The very presence of the Spirit of God in our hearts is the promise that we shall dwell with Him throughout eternity. When He comes into our lives, He is the "down payment," as it were, that eternity in glory is ours. "In whom ye also trusted, after that ye heard the word of truth, the gospel of your salvation: in whom also having believed, ye were sealed with the holy Spirit of promise, which is the down payment of our inheritance" is the literal meaning of Ephesians 1:13, 14. The Holy Spirit is the seal of God's ownership. He will not break His seal. Our salvation depends on God's faithfulness and not on ours. Assurance of salvation depends on God's keeping power and not on

The Holy Spirit seals the believer

our "hanging-on" power or our feelings. Jesus said: "And I give unto them eternal life; and they shall *never perish*" (John 10:28).

Too many people are looking for some emotional experience or some hilarious feeling to make them "feel saved." But we are saved by receiving a Saviour and not by feeling something. As we walk in fellowship with God we will surely feel the peace and joy of assurance, but it is a result of salvation and not a means of salvation.

VI. The Holy Spirit Guides the Believer

Jesus said: "Howbeit when he, the Spirit of truth, is come, he will guide you into all truth" (John 16:13).

Instead of depending on visions and dreams and voices today, we have the Word of God to guide us. The Holy Spirit speaks to us through His Word. The guidance of God comes only when we spend time in His Word and

The Holy Spirit guides the believer

prayer. The answers are all in the miracle Book, but we have to know where to find them. To neglect the Bible is one sure way not to be led by the Spirit. Jesus said: "Search the scriptures . . . they are they which testify of me" (John 5:39). "For as many as are led by the Spirit of God, they are the sons of God" (Rom. 8:14).

God never tells us to do anything that is contrary to the principles of the Bible.

A young Christian man came asking advice. "How can I know God's will for my life?"

"What career do you have in mind?" I asked.

"Well, I want to go to Hollywood and act," he spoke a little ashamedly, "but my parents say a Hollywood movie community is godless, and that the movies do not glorify God." He put out his chin. "But they are so old-fashioned. I'm young! There's nothing in the Bible against acting in Hollywood!"

"Do you think Hollywood glorifies God according to the truth?" I asked.

He hung his head, "No, I guess not."

"Well, the Scripture says: 'Whether therefore ye eat or drink, or whatsoever ye do [and that includes acting in Hollywood!], do all to the glory of God.' So if you really want to know God's will for your life, it's very clear, isn't it?" I asked.

That young man is now studying for the ministry. He decided that God could use his talents better than Hollywood could!

VII. The Holy Spirit Fills the Consecrated Believer

God says: "Be filled with the Spirit" (Eph. 5:18-20). This is a command, not just a suggestion! This is also the normal Christian life and not just a mountain-peak experience. To be Spirit-filled is to be Spirit-controlled. It means that His hand is on the wheel and His will is our desire.

But how can we be Spirit-filled?

How can a bottle be filled with air if it is filled with

THE EMPTY BOTTLE IS THE ONE
FILLED WITH AIR

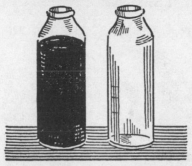

ink? Simply empty out the ink! You do not have to use a pump to pump air into the bottle, just empty it, and it is filled!

When we confess and forsake sin we are filled with the Spirit of God. A Spirit-filled life is an obedient life to the Word of God; it is a victorious life over sin; it is a yielded life to the will of God. Do not forget, though, this is the *normal* Christian life. Too often people think that those who are living close to God are fanatics or freaks. But the freak is the one who is not filled with the Spirit of God!

Romans 12:1, 2 says literally: "I beg of you therefore, Christians, because of the mercies of God, that ye present your bodies a living sacrifice [a 'sacrifice' is that which is given over to the use of another], holy, acceptable unto God [only a holy sacrifice is acceptable unto God], which is your intelligent service [there's no blind ignorance in Christian service]. And be not poured into the same mold as this sinful world: but be ye transfigured with a changed appearance, by the making new of your mind and soul, that ye may experience what is that good, and acceptable, and perfect, will of God."

There can be only one throne in the Christian's life. The throne stands for Lordship. "Confess with thy mouth Jesus as Lord" (Rom. 10:9).

WHO OCCUPIES THE THRONE

There must be a cross in each of our lives too. It is not an ornament to wear or carry, but a life of self-denial that Christ refers to when He says: "Whosoever will come after me, let him deny himself, and take up his cross, and follow me" (Mark 8:34). There can't be two lords of our lives; one has to be put down, and that one should be "I." If I want Christ to be on the throne of my life, then "I" must be on the cross. If I want to be on the throne myself, then I am crucifying afresh the Son of God.

Just what does all this mean in everyday English? It means simply that if I am Spirit-filled, I will want Christ to be the one to control my life and I will count myself out. There cannot be two "bosses"; either I obey Christ, or I disobey Him. If I obey Him, then He is my Lord as well as my Saviour; if I disobey Him, then I shame Him and admit that I want to rule my own life—I am not Spirit-filled.

Here again we do not need to agonize and emotionalize to be filled with the Holy Spirit. He waits to fill us. We need but to confess our sin and take our hands off, and He will take over.

When sin comes into our lives, we are no longer Spirit-controlled.

Surrender sin and self to Him, and He will take over. We do this just as we surrender our hearts to Him when we are saved—*ask* Him to cleanse and control.

VIII. The Holy Spirit Empowers Those Who Serve Him

Jesus said: "But ye shall receive power, after that the Holy Ghost is come upon you: and ye shall be witnesses unto me" (Acts 1:8). The power of the Spirit is given to those who are serving Him and doing His will. Like

The Holy Spirit empowers believers

POWER

a fire or electricity that generates power, the Holy Spirit is the source of victory over sin and conviction of sin in the lives of sinners. This power of God is available when we need Him to help us overcome sin or to convict those we are dealing with of their need of a Saviour. Here again, we do not need to pray and pray for God to do what He is just waiting to do. We simply claim His power and go forward to deal with souls. To ask for the power of God when we are making no effort to win souls is to insult God!

We have never been promised the power of God so that we might experience some feeling or emotion ourselves. Instead, the power of God is felt in the heart of the one we deal with, so that he feels conviction. The soul-winner may not feel any emotional upheaval, but the one he witnesses to will ask, "What must I do to be saved?"

Those who try to reproduce the phenomenon in the Book of Acts must remember that those who sinned against God in those days fell dead and were eaten by worms! It was a drastic time of signs and miracles to produce fear in the hearts of unbelieving Jews. Thank God, we are now in the day of grace and we have the Word of God to guide us and the Spirit of God to do His office work, and need not the physical signs and demonstrations then given for the infant church!

IX. Sins Against the Holy Spirit

A. RESISTING THE HOLY SPIRIT. Not to respond to the convicting voice of the Spirit of God is to resist Him. There is no halfway course. Either we receive Him or reject Him. God will not always continue knocking at unbelievers' hearts. He says: "My spirit shall not always strive with man" (Gen. 6:3). In fact, the only time we can count our own is right *now*. We have no assurance of tomorrow. "Behold, now is the accepted time; behold, now is the day of salvation" (II Cor. 6:2).

The final rejection of the Saviour is called the "unpardonable sin." It is unpardonable because there is no other Sacrifice for and Saviour from sin. "For if we sin willfully [purposefully reject the Saviour] after that we have received the knowledge of the truth, there remaineth no more sacrifice for sins, but a certain fearful looking for of judgment and fiery indignation, which shall devour

the adversaries" (Heb. 10:26, 27) . The work of the Holy Spirit is to convict men of their need of a Saviour from sin. To "blaspheme" is to reject the only Saviour for sins, so there is no other one to forgive sins (Matt. 12: 31, 32) .

A minister told me of his experience with a man who refused to accept Christ as Saviour. During evangelistic meetings in their church that man was greatly under conviction, but he would not respond to the invitation for salvation. It was during the last night's meeting that the man literally shook with conviction. Still he would not accept the Lord. Eventually, he strode out of the church, slamming the door behind him. He never came back. From that day on his whole nature seemed to change.

Three weeks later he lay on his deathbed. The doctors were nonplused, "We can find nothing organically wrong," they said.

The minister went to call and the man spoke up, "Preacher," he said, "you're wasting your time with me. That day when I walked out of the church I decided once and for all that religion was not for me. Something seemed to die within me. My heart turned to stone. I couldn't be saved now even if I were interested." He died with these words on his lips.

If you have not accepted Christ as your personal Saviour, you are in danger of committing this unpardonable sin. Do not take a chance on tomorrow. The very fact that you are concerned about the subject shows that you have not yet driven the Spirit of God away. Those who have committed the unpardonable sin lose their conviction of sin and cease to care. Why not ask Him to take over your life right now, and settle the matter once and for all?

B. GRIEVING THE HOLY SPIRIT. "Grieve not the holy Spirit of God" (Eph. 4:30-32). When believers fall into sin, they grieve their heavenly Father. The fact that God will always judge sin in the lives of His children is reason enough why we should not want to sin. But trouble is not the only result of sin—the saddest thing of all is that sin grieves the heart of God.

The realization of the indwelling Holy Spirit should make us very conscious of sin, and very desirous not to grieve Him.

C. QUENCHING THE HOLY SPIRIT. "Quench not the Spirit" (I Thess. 5:19). The Spirit of God is likened to a fire that refines and empowers. When we allow sin to remain in our lives, it is as if we were pouring water on the power of God. True, the Holy Spirit never leaves us once we have received Him, but we do not get away with sin. What we sow, that we shall reap.

"Behold, the Lord's hand is not shortened, that it cannot save; neither his ear heavy, that it cannot hear: but your iniquities have separated between you and your God, and your sins have hid his face from you, that he will not hear" (Isa. 59:1, 2). When we allow unconfessed sin in our lives, we not only grieve the Holy Spirit, but

we also hinder His answering our prayers; we cut off His blessing; we cause others to stumble, and we lose our reward in Heaven.

I knew a church member who drifted into a life of worldliness. He and his family had been very regular in the house of God until his business began to prosper beyond belief. With prosperity came backsliding. He tossed off the warnings given him by saying, "Why, I've never been so prosperous! God is blessing me as never before!"

Then came the day when he stopped coming to church. He gave the excuse that he was too busy. But he was not too busy to frequent the taverns in company with careless women.

Soon his boys dropped out of church; instead, they too frequented the taverns. Then his wife no longer came to church; not because she was backsliding; she died of a broken heart.

Yes, that Christian eventually came back to church. But not until his business had folded up, disaster after disaster had wiped it out. His boys were juvenile delinquents; his wife dead. He came back—but alone.

"Quench not the Spirit!" "Grieve not the holy Spirit!"

How dangerous it is to tempt the patience of God! Is there sin in your life? Are you grieving and quenching the Holy Spirit? Are you seeing the power of God unfurled on your behalf in winning others, or are you drifting along in a defeated half-mast Christian life?

Now is not only the time to receive the Saviour; it is also the time to confess and forsake sin and realize the power and filling of God for living, serving, and victory.

QUESTIONS

1. Who is the Holy Spirit? (Acts 5:3, 4; John 14:16, 17).

2. Did the Holy Spirit forever abide in the hearts of Old Testament saints? (Ps. 51:11).

3. Why did God give signs and miracles at the beginning of the Church Age? (Heb. 2:3, 4).

4. What languages were spoken by those who spoke in tongues? (Acts 2:8-11)

5. What is the message of the Holy Spirit? (John 16:13, 14)

6. Why can't the unsaved understand the Bible? (I Cor. 2:14)

7. What is the work of the Holy Spirit in regard to the unsaved? (John 16:8, 9; Rev. 3:20)

8. Why can we be righteous? (John 16:8, 9; Heb. 7:25)

9. How long will the Holy Spirit remain with the believer? (John 14:16, 17)

10. Where does God dwell today? (I Cor. 6:19, 20)

11. How can we have victory over sin? (John 16:11; I Cor. 15:57)

12. What proof do we have that we are saved? (Eph. 1: 13, 14; 4:30)

13. How does God guide believers today? (John 16:13)

14. What is the normal Christian life? (Eph. 5:18-20)

15. How can we know the will of God? (Rom. 12:1, 2)

16. What is the purpose of the power of the Spirit? (Acts 1:8)

17. What is the unpardonable sin? (Matt. 12:31, 32; Heb. 10:26-29)

18. How does one grieve the Holy Spirit? (Eph. 4:30-32)

19. What hinders the power of God? (Isa. 59:1, 2)

20. Does God remain knocking at the hearts of sinners forever? (Gen. 6:3)

4

THE SIN QUESTION

THERE SEEMS TO BE MUCH DEBATE about this question. Everyone wishes to set his own standard of what he considers right or wrong. Some deny the subject altogether and insist that there is no such thing as sin. If this is true, then God made a mistake when saying there is sin. If there is no sin, then why does God speak about the wages of sin? If there is no sin, why did God send His Son to die for sin?

The best way to answer the question is to see what God says about it in His Word, the Bible.

A simple definition for sin might be: "Sin is disobedience to God; sin is self-will against God's will."

But first of all, just where did sin originate? God is the Creator of all; did He create sin? Certainly not! Sin is the one thing God did not create.

At one time there was no sin. God reigned supreme among the angels in glory. His chief minister was a personage called Lucifer, or Satan. Isaiah 14:12-17 tells of Lucifer's desire to take God's place, and pit his own will against the will of God. Sin was born in Satan when he said, "I will be like the most High." Ezekiel 28:15 says: "Thou wast perfect in thy ways from the day that thou wast created, till iniquity was found in thee."

The only thing Satan has ever created is sin; and sin is self-will against God's will. Satan was cast out of Heaven with his followers, and his fall, no doubt, destroyed the world that God had made. "And the earth *became* without form and void" (Gen. 1:2).

When God created mankind, Satan was once more on hand to try to ruin this creation. He succeeded, because Adam and Eve chose *self-will* instead of God's will, and sin was born in the human race. From then on the entire human race inherited a sinful nature. "In sin did my mother conceive me" (Ps. 51:5). This does not mean that conception is sin, but that we are conceived by sinful parents.

This sinful nature is only too evident even in newborn babies when they give vent to temper and impatience!

A young mother was indignant at the thought that her child had a sinful nature. "Do you mean to tell me that my darling has a sinful nature?" she demanded. "Why, look at her, she's just precious!"

Just then "little precious" kicked her mother on the shins. In a flash the mother slapped her soundly, scolding, "You little dickens, you!"

"Little precious" had suddenly become "little dickens"!

But not only is the human race constituted sinners by nature, we are also sinners by practice. As soon as we are old enough to be intellectually responsible, we are accountable for sin. And *no* one is exempt.

"They are all under sin . . . none righteous, no, not one . . . all gone out of the way . . . there is none that doeth good, no, not one . . . all the world may become guilty before God . . . there is no difference: for *all have sinned*" (Rom. 3:9-23).

All is *all,* including you and me! You cannot add anything to all, nor take anything away from all. No matter how we try to whitewash sin by mild names such as mistakes, faults, slips, failures, the fact remains that we are sinners.

"All we like sheep have gone astray; we have turned everyone to his *own way*" (Isa. 53:6). That is the problem right there—self-will! "For all have sinned, and come short of the glory of God" (Rom. 3:23). God demands perfection. Not even one sin can enter His presence. We have all come short of this standard of perfection. Oh,

yes, some might come "shorter" than others, but we cannot compare ourselves with others, we have *all* come short.

Though some might try to stand on the ladder of education or on the pedestal of respectability and think they are higher than others, they still come short of perfection

I. Definition of Sin

Now let us look at some Bible definitions of sin.

A. "ALL UNRIGHTEOUSNESS IS SIN" (I John 5:17). It does not say how great unrighteousness. *Any* speck of sin, *any* measure of imperfection, *any* failure, is sin. God does not grade sin as our social system grades sin. The farmer grades his potatoes into large baking potatoes, medium sized for boiling, and tiny ones he feeds to the pigs. Men think of murder as a great sin, stealing as a

lesser sin, and little white lies do not count! But with God all sin is sin.

B. "SIN IS THE TRANSGRESSION OF THE LAW" (I John 3: 4). *Transgress* means to step out of bounds, or to step over the line, to trespass. It does not say how far over the line. When we see a sign that says, "No Trespassing," it does not matter if we walk a mile or just take one step over the fence, we are trespassing.

In the contest for a prize, the archer who tries for the bull's-eye and misses by an inch fails to win the prize for the same reason as the archer who misses by a long-shot— both missed the bull's-eye. To sin is to miss the mark of God's requirement.

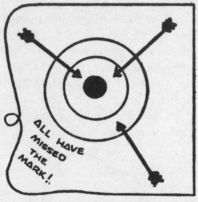

ALL HAVE MISSED THE MARK!

"Whosoever shall keep the whole law, and yet offend in one point, he is guilty of all" (James 2:10). The God who said, "Thou shalt not kill," also said, "Thou shalt not commit adultery." He who said, "Thou shalt not kill," also said, "Forsaking not the assembling of yourselves together" for worship. He who said, "Thou shalt not bear false witness," also said, "Search the scriptures." It is not a matter of which command we disobey; all are God's commands, and to disobey any one of them is *sin*.

It only takes one hole to sink a canoe, one bullet in the heart will kill; one broken link in a chain will let the load fall; one murder makes a murderer.

It is possible to be very sincere in religion, and yet to be sincerely wrong! Traveling home from a speaking appointment one night I was driving along in good faith hoping to get home soon and to bed because I was very tired. I noticed a sign along the highway that said I was nearing a town that was in the opposite direction than I thought I was going. I slowed down to get my bearings. The sign must be wrong, I decided, and I looked at the sky to check my directions. Lo and behold, I was going due north instead of due south! I was sincere enough to argue that I was right, but I was sincerely wrong!

C. "WHATSOEVER IS NOT OF FAITH IS SIN" (Rom. 14:23). Doubt against God's Word is sin. Unbelief in the Saviour and His promises of power to keep—this is the sin that damns men. "Of sin, because they believe not on me" (John 16:9). The Bible does not teach mortal or venial sin. *All sin is sin;* there is no difference with God.

II. What Is the Result of Sin?

"The wages of sin is death" (Rom. 6:23). "The soul that sinneth, it shall die" (Ezek. 18:20).

The word *death* means "separation." There are three kinds of death as a result of sin.

A. PHYSICAL DEATH. The separation of the person from body is called death. Physical death is a result of sin.

B. SPIRITUAL DEATH. The separation of the sinner from the presence and fellowship of God is called spiritual death. Because of sin, the sinner has no connection with

God and has no access to God; he is called the enemy of God, alien from God, and is "dead in trespasses and sins" (Eph. 2:1-3, 12).

As the electric light bulb has light only when it is connected with the electric source, so we have spiritual life only when we are connected with God. When the connection is broken, the bulb goes out; when sin comes into the life of the sinner, he is said to be dead in sins. The only remedy is to mend a break and restore the connection. Christ is the only One who can mend this break between the sinner and God, "Christ died for our sins."

North, south, east and west—the world is filled with people who are physically alive, yet spiritual corpses, dead in sins. When Adam and Eve sinned they did not immediately fall down and die physically, but they did break their fellowship with God, and they died spiritually. That fellowship was later restored.

C. ETERNAL DEATH. The eternal separation from God in the lake of fire is the final destination of the sinner. This is called the "second death." "The lake which burneth with fire and brimstone: which is the second death" (Rev. 20:14, 15; 21:8).

God is holy, completely and entirely holy. "God is light and in him is no darkness at all" (I John 1:5). No sin can enter His presence, not even one lie. "And there shall in no wise enter into it [heaven] anything that defileth, neither whatsoever worketh abomination, or maketh a lie" (Rev. 21:27).

It makes a hopeless picture, does it not? But until we realize that our condition is hopeless, there is no remedy. God's remedy is for *sinners*. Those who do not realize their sin do not feel their need of a Saviour. The first step of salvation is the admission that we are lost.

The sin that sends a man to Hell is the sin of neglecting the remedy God offers for sin. A dying man who is offered a sure cure for his illness, but neglects to take the cure, will die. The cause of death would be the failure to take the remedy.

III. What Is the Remedy for Sin?

Men have tried to invent their own remedies for sin. Not willing to take God's way of salvation, and not willing to admit that they are sinners and unable to help themselves, lost sinners have made their own rules. Do

TURNING OVER A NEW LEAF DOES NOT ERASE THE PAST—

any of the following sound familiar? Keep the golden rule! Do the best you can! Turn over a new leaf! Keep the commandments!

None of these rules will take away sin. "By the deeds of the law there shall no flesh be justified" (Rom. 3:20). "A man is not justified by the works of the law" (Gal. 2:16). "Not by works of righteousness which we have done, but according to his mercy he saved us" (Titus 3:5). "Not of works, lest any man should boast" (Eph. 2:9).

Trying to be good will not take away the sins of the past. Turning over a new leaf does not blot out the mistakes of the past. It is impossible for a sinner to be good; even his efforts of being good are repugnant to God, "all our righteousnesses are as filthy rags" (Isa. 64:6).

A. GOD'S REMEDY IS A SAVIOUR TO TAKE SIN AWAY. Even though God demands the death penalty for sin, His love yearns to save the sinner. The only answer is to find someone who could take the death penalty for the guilty sinner. This someone must have no sin. There is only One who could fill the need, Jesus Christ, God's own Son. "As it is appointed unto men once to die, but after this the judgment: so Christ was once offered to bear the sins of many" (Heb. 9:27, 28).

The sacrifices in the Old Testament were an illustration of Christ, the Lamb of God who taketh away the sins of the world. Those sacrifices could never take away sin, but they pointed by faith to the Saviour that should come. "And every priest standeth daily ministering and offering oftentimes the same sacrifices, which can never take away sins" (Heb. 10:11). "For the law having a shadow of good things to come . . . can never with those sacrifices which they offered year by year continually make the comers thereunto perfect" (Heb. 10:1). Without Christ the Old Testament rituals have no meaning. The Temple, the tabernacle, the sacrifices, and holy things are all explained in Christ.

The Jews who reject Christ as their Messiah have no real meaning to their Scriptures. "But their minds were blinded: for until this day remaineth the same veil untaken away in the reading of the Old Testament; which veil is done away in Christ. But even unto this day, when Moses is read, the veil is upon their heart. Nevertheless when it [Israel] shall turn to the Lord, the veil shall be taken away" (II Cor. 3:14-16).

B. CHRIST ALONE IS THE SIN-BEARER FOR THE SINS OF ALL. Christ's substitutionary death is sufficient for the sins of the whole world, for He is God. As God, His sufferings on the cross as the Sin-bearer was equivalent to an eternity in Hell. His cry, "My God, my God, why hast thou forsaken me?" was the agonized cry of a holy Son separated from His holy Father, something that we sinners can never fully appreciate. "For he [God] hath made him [Christ] to be sin for us, who knew no sin; that we might be made the righteousness of God in him" (II Cor. 5:21).

Even though the death of Christ is sufficient for the whole world, it is *efficient* only for those who receive Him as their personal Saviour from sin. When we let Christ take our sin away, we stand before God as sinless. Christ becomes our Substitute. "The Lord hath laid on him the iniquity of us all" (Isa. 53:6). "Who his own self bare our sins in his own body on the tree, that we, being dead to sins, should live unto righteousness: by whose stripes ye were healed" (I Peter 2:24).

Christ takes our sin away so that we should live unto righteousness.

Speaking in a church one Sunday night, I was conscious of a tenseness in the congregation but did not understand the reason. At the invitation for those who would receive Christ as their Saviour to come forward, a weeping woman arose, came forward and knelt by the platform. Several others came forward too, but I could see the church was visibly affected by that one woman's response. A few moments later a man arose from the other side of the church and came down to the front with the tears rolling down his face. He knelt beside the weeping woman and put his arm around her shoulders.

That couple had been on the verge of divorce; they were alcoholics. Their Christian daughter and the church friends had been praying for them, and that night friends had brought them to the meeting. They met in reconciliation at the feet of the Saviour.

I heard from them a year later: "This last year has been Heaven in our home!" When the Saviour came into their lives, sin went out.

C. CHRIST IS THE SIN-BEARER FOR ALL SIN. "The blood of Jesus Christ his Son cleanseth us from all sin" (I John 1:7). "Without shedding of blood is no remission" (Heb.

9:22). Penance does not take away sin; the fire of purgatory will not take away sin. The Bible does not teach a purgatory after death. The one place where sins are purged away is on the cross of Calvary. "When he [Christ] had by himself purged our sins" (Heb. 1:3). There are no sins that the blood of Christ cannot wash away. "If we confess our sins *he* [Christ] is faithful and just to forgive us our sins, and to cleanse us from *all* unrighteousness" (I John 1:9).

There is no need for anyone or anything else to remove sin. There is only one Mediator between God and man, and that is the man, Christ Jesus (I Tim. 2:5). One who claims to have the power to represent God in forgiving sins should also have the power to cast out demons and raise the dead! (Matt. 10:5-8). "Who can forgive sins but God only." "Unto him that loved us, and washed us from our sins in his own blood . . . be glory and dominion forever and ever. Amen" (Rev. 1:5, 6).

IV. How Can We Receive This Remedy for Sin?

The Saviour is provided, the pardon is available, the way to God is open. "Neither is there salvation in any other: for there is none other name under heaven, given

among men, whereby we must be saved" (Acts 4:12).
"Whosoever shall call upon the name of the Lord shall
be saved" (Rom. 10:13). "But as many as received him,
to them gave he power to become the sons of God" (John
1:12).

Our part is to accept the Saviour. Salvation is the gift
of God; it is for us to accept it, and then live a life of
thanksgiving and thanksliving. *Receive* means to *accept,*
to take Christ.

It was after the preaching in the tent meetings in the
Philippines that a local merchant came to inquire about
salvation. He had been attending the meetings for several weeks, so I asked him, "Do you understand that
when you ask Christ to be your Saviour that He will
save you from sin as well as from Hell?"

"Yes, I understand," he replied, "I have been hearing
the teaching for many nights."

"Then do you want Him to save you from sin?" I tried
to make it hard for him.

He hesitated. "But ma'am, is my drinking a sin? Is
my gambling a sin? Is my smoking a sin?"

"Do you think they are?" I asked.

He looked worried, for like most Filipinos he had done
these things since his childhood. Then he mumbled,
"Yes, I think they are!"

"Then do you want Christ to save you from your sin?"

His head came up with a smile, "Yes, I am willing."

We prayed together, and he said his first prayer, "Please
God, save me from all my sin and from my tobacco, my
gambling, and my liquor. Amen." His smile was a joy
to behold. But the smile faded as he pondered, "But
ma'am, if I put these things out of my life, what about
my business? I sell these things in my store!"

"That is indeed your business," I replied, "you must
settle that with the Lord."

Well, his wife was the storekeeper; he was only the owner! And she was exceedingly antagonistic. The husband returned home with his glowing testimony and announced, "I have received Jesus Christ as my Saviour from Hell and from sin. Now we will put the liquor and tobacco out of the store!"

"No, we will not!" the wife was very adamant.

"Yes, we will!" he was equally determined.

For a week they quarreled until he could stand it no longer. He found out that he was not the head of his house!

"Very well, then," he finally declared, "if you do not want me to be good and have my Jesus, then I will be bad like I used to be!" He tore up his Bible and threw the pieces around the house, rushed down to the market and got drunk and started a fist fight.

His wife came running down to the market, calling, "Come home, come home! You can do as you want and have your Jesus, but do not be bad like you used to be!" That night he came back to the meetings and bought a new Bible!

How well I remember the day he was baptized! Coming out of the water with that wonderful smile, he shook hands with us and said, "Thank you for bringing Jesus to my town. I have tried many religions, but not until now have I found satisfaction for the hunger of my heart!"

He went home to his wife, and knelt before her, pleading, "Will you not receive Jesus Christ as your Saviour?" The tears came to her eyes and she said, "Why do you ask me this when I am so cross with you always?"

"Because I love my Jesus I love you too!" he replied.

A year later that wife came to know Christ and gave her heart to God, and she testified, "The life of my husband was so changed that I knew he had found the truth."

Too often people forget that Christ is the Saviour from sin as well as from Hell. "His name shall be called Jesus, for he shall save his people from their sins" (Matt. 1:21).

V. What Is the Result of Receiving Christ as Personal Saviour?

Christ says, "Go, and sin no more!" (John 8:11). His will is that we live a life of righteousness. "These things write I unto you, that ye sin not" (I John 2:1). There is no use saying we want to be saved if we want to keep our sin.

However, that does not mean that we will never fall into sin again. We are still human beings! I'm glad that I John 2:1 continues with: "and if any man sin, we have an advocate with the Father, Jesus Christ the righteous." No, we are not perfect, but we *want to be*. That is the difference between a saved sinner and a lost sinner. One loves sin, the other hates sin.

Christ is not only the Saviour, He is also the Advocate. A lawyer must be the friend of the government and a friend of the sinner, and he must be innocent of the crime. Only Christ can fill this requirement.

Notice the next verse too: "And he is the propitiation for our sins: and not for ours only, but also for the sins of the whole world." *Propitiation* means to turn away wrath. As the guilty sinner stands condemned before a

holy God, he can expect only judgment and wrath to fall on him. But when he accepts Christ as his Saviour, the wrath of God falls on Christ, and the sinner is not condemned. Christ stands between him and God!

Every day of his life, the saved sinner wants to keep in fellowship with God. When he sins, he immediately confesses and forsakes that sin and the fellowship is restored. "He that covereth his sin shall not prosper, but he that confesseth and forsaketh it shall have mercy" (Prov. 28: 13). That is the secret of forgiveness—*forsake sin*. Too many people think that to confess sin means merely to recite it, and then go out and do the same thing again. To confess sin means to admit it is sin, to hate it as God hates it, and to forsake it.

There is a verse especially for believers. "Therefore to him that knoweth to do good, and doeth it not, to him it is sin" (James 4:17). Sin is not just doing evil; it is also failing to do good. There are sins of omission as well as commission. A saved sinner, who knows God's will and does not do it, is living in sin. "And that servant, which knew his lord's will, and prepared not himself, neither did according to his will, shall be beaten with many stripes" (Luke 12:47).

The sin of *neglect* is as bad as the sin of wrongdoing. Obedience to the Word of God is as important as keeping from evil.

It was in a church that considered itself especially spiritual that God recently brought real conviction of sin. I felt directed to apply the message to Christians because that church seldom had visitors. As I spoke I could see that God was striking home to hearts, and instead of closing the service I asked the pastor to take over. I can still hear his words. "We as a church have failed. We have been so occupied with not doing wrong, that we have perhaps failed to do good and reach our unsaved neighbors. I confess my own sin. . . ." He broke down before God. One after another of his people prayed to confess sin with tears of repentance. A revival had begun. Backsliders came back to God, young people surrendered their lives for full-time service for God

Christians, are we living in the sin of omission? Not to witness for Christ is as great a sin as murder; not to pray is as bad as witchcraft; not to worship is as bad as idolatry. Sin is disobedience to God no matter what form it takes.

"Let not sin therefore reign in your mortal body, that ye should obey it in the lusts thereof. Neither yield ye your members as instruments of unrighteousness unto sin: but yield yourselves unto God, as those that are alive from the dead, and your members as instruments of righteousness unto God" (Rom. 6:12, 13).

QUESTIONS

1. Where did sin begin? (Isa. 14:12-17)
2. What was Satan's original state? (Ezek. 28:12-15)
3. When do men receive a sinful nature? (Ps. 51:5)
4. Who are sinners? (Rom. 3:23)
5. Did Mary the mother of Jesus ever sin? (Rom. 3: 10-12)
6. How much unrighteousness makes us sinners? (I John 5:17)
7. How many sins condemn us? (James 2:10)
8. What is sin? (John 16:9)
9. What is the result of sin? (Rom. 6:23)
10. What is spiritual death? (Eph. 2:1-3)
11. What is the second death? (Rev. 20:14)
12. Can reform or good works take away our sin? (Rom. 3:20; Titus 3:5)
13. Can we please God as long as our sins are not forgiven? (Isa. 64:6)
14. What is the only thing that can take away sin? (Heb. 9:22, 27, 28)
15. Who is the only sin-bearer? (I Peter 2:24)
16. Who can forgive sins? (I John 1:9; Rev. 1:5)
17. What is the result of sins forgiven? (I John 2:1)
18. What does sincere confession include? (Prov. 28:13)
19. What is as bad as doing wrong? (James 4:17)
20. What is the result of a Christian's sins? (Luke 12:47)

5

THE NEW BIRTH

IT IS SURPRISING how many people think that they are the children of God just because they are members of the human race. True enough that God created each of us so that we are His creation, but when it comes to being the children of God spiritually, He says: ". . . they which are the children of the flesh, these are not the children of God" (Rom. 9:8).

There are two families in the world—not the Smiths and Browns—but the family of God and the family of sin. "In this the children of God are manifest, and the children of the devil" (I John 3:10).

In John 3 we read of a man called Nicodemus, a religious leader of the Jews, who no doubt wanted to find out if Jesus was really the Messiah or not. The Jews were looking for a king who would deliver them from the tyranny of Rome and set up the kingdom in Jerusalem. Nicodemus came to Jesus by night as a precaution. He did not want to cast his lot with any group that was not going to be the winning team. But Jesus knew what was in his mind, and came right to the point by saying: "Except a man be born again [from above], he cannot see the kingdom of God" (John 3:3).

Nicodemus was naturally curious, and asked, "How can a man be born when he is old?" He did not understand that Jesus was speaking of a spiritual birth and not just a physical birth. Christ then made it clear that this has nothing to do with physical things, by saying: "That which is born of the flesh is flesh; and that which is born of the Spirit is spirit."

But why should this religious man be born from above? He was a good man, a leader of his people, and a Pharisee. He was no down-and-out!

He needed to be born again for the same reason that you and I do—because Jesus said so! But there are other reasons too.

I. Why Should We Be Born Again?

A. WE ARE IN THE WRONG FAMILY. "The children of disobedience . . . were by nature the children of wrath" (Eph. 2:2, 3).

This is not speaking of small children. Babies have a sinful nature when they are born, but they are not accountable for sin until they are old enough to understand. Once they reach the age of accountability, they are sinners by nature and sinners by practice, and are responsible for their actions. Jesus said to those who had not believed in Him: "Ye are of your father the devil, and the lusts of your father ye will do" (John 8:44).

The Bible indicates that small children belong to God and go to Heaven when they die. "Except ye be con-

SATAN'S FAMILY

"Ye are of your father the devil."

verted, and become as little children, ye shall not enter into the kingdom of heaven" (Matt. 18:3). "Take heed that ye despise not one of these little ones . . . in heaven their angels do always behold the face of my Father which is in heaven" (Matt. 18:10). Angels are assigned to minister to those who shall be heirs of salvation (Heb. 1:14).

"Even so it is not the will of your Father which is in heaven, that one of these little ones should perish" (Matt. 18:14). "But Jesus said, Suffer little children, and forbid them not, to come unto me: for of such is the kingdom of heaven" (Matt. 19:14).

God does not condemn anyone to Hell who is not mentally capable of understanding spiritual things. "Shall not the Judge of all the earth do right?" (Gen. 18:25).

You who can read these words, you are old enough to be accountable for sin, so there is no excuse for you!

B. WE LIVE THE WRONG KIND OF LIFE. "Ye are of your father the devil, and the lusts of your father ye will do" (John 8:44). A life of disobedience to God is the consequence of being in the wrong family; we are aliens from God. God is not our Father but our Judge. We are lost, condemned.

God says: "He that believeth not is condemned already. . . . The wrath of God abideth on him" (John 3: 18, 36).

Just as a condemned man in the death cell waits for execution, so we are condemned already and wait only the final day of judgment. Although the criminal might be physically alive, if he has been found guilty and sentenced to death, he is a dead man as far as the law is concerned. Those who have been found guilty by the Almighty Judge and condemned to Hell might still be physically alive, but are dead in trespasses and sins as far as God is concerned. There is nothing we can do to excuse or pardon ourselves any more than a murderer can expect leniency or pardon just because he promises never to kill again. Reform is not the answer to the problem; it is too late; we are condemned already.

"He that committeth sin is of the devil" (I John 3:8). We need to be born again!

C. WE HAVE THE WRONG DESTINATION. "For the wrath of God is revealed from heaven against all ungodliness and unrighteousness of men" (Rom. 1:18). "In flaming fire taking vengeance on them that know not God, and that obey not the gospel of our Lord Jesus Christ: who shall be punished with everlasting destruction from the presence of the Lord" (II Thess. 1:8, 9). When we remain in Satan's family we shall have to go along with him some day. Hell was not made for men, but for the Devil and his angels. However, if we have not been born again, we go with our father the Devil. "And the devil that deceived them was cast into the lake of fire and brimstone . . . and shall be tormented day and night forever and ever" (Rev. 20:10). "And whosoever was not found written in the book of life was cast into the lake of fire" (Rev. 20:15).

"But the fearful, and unbelieving, and the abominable, and murderers, and whoremongers, and sorcerers, and idolaters, and all liars, shall have their part in the lake which burneth with fire and brimstone: which is the second death" (Rev. 21:8).

II. How We Are Not Born Again

A. NOT BY MEANS OF HUMAN PARENTS. "Which were born, *not of blood*" (John 1:13). Just because we have Christian parents it does not mean that we are the children of God. Human blood gives us no priority with

God. This is a *spiritual birth;* we are not born again by human or physical means or agents. "They which are the children of the flesh, these are not the children of God" (Rom. 9:8).

B. NOT BY OUR OWN EFFORTS OR DEEDS. "Nor of the *will of the flesh*" (John 1:13). Nothing that we can do or be will please God until we are born again. The spiritual birth is a gift of God, and not earned by doing good deeds. "Not by works of righteousness which we have done" (Titus 3:5). "Not of works, lest any man should boast" (Eph. 2:8, 9). We cannot live a *good* life until we belong to God's family.

C. NOT BY ANYTHING THAT ANY MAN CAN DO FOR US. "Nor of the *will of man,* but of God" (John 1:13). Nothing that any church can do for us; nothing that a preacher, priest, or missionary can do for us will make us a child of God. No ritual, no baptism, no confirmation, no communion, nothing can make us a child of God *except receiving Christ as our personal Saviour.*

III. How Can We Be Born Again?

"But as many as received him [Christ] to them gave he power [the right] to become the sons of God, even to them that believe on his name" (John 1:12). The new birth is the act of receiving a Saviour. God hates sin, but He loves the sinner. His love provided a Saviour to take away sins. "For God so loved the world, that he gave his only begotten Son, that whosoever believeth in him should not perish, but have everlasting life" (John 3:16).

Since God demands the death penalty for sin, the only way that the justice of God can be satisfied is for the sinner to spend eternity in Hell, or for someone to die as his substitute. "God commendeth his love toward us, in that, while we were yet sinners, Christ died for us" (Rom. 5:8).

The story is told of a man who was found guilty of a crime and condemned to die. He languished in the death cell waiting for the day of execution and worried about his wife and children who would be left unprovided for. But he had a friend. This friend was an unmarried young man. He went to the judge and offered to take the death penalty that the husband and father might go free. The judge searched the books of the law and found that the crime had to be punished by death, but he said to the young man, "If you are willing to pay the penalty, the law will be satisfied." On the day of execution that young man died in the place of his friend. The prisoner returned to his wife and family with tears of gratitude to live a life that was exemplary in the community, saying, "Because my friend died for me, I want to live a life that is worthy of him!"

That story, however, is inadequate to illustrate what Christ did for us. He died for His enemies while that young man died for his friend. Christ's sacrifice is beyond the understanding of our human minds. How could He love us when we are so unlovely! "Behold, what manner of love the Father hath bestowed upon us, that we should be called the sons of God" (I John 3:1).

A man in the death cell might hope to gain release by offering money, but God cannot be bribed! The condemned criminal might hope for reprieve by good behavior, but if he is condemned already, even good behavior will not clear the slate. He needs a substitute.

Notice again the words in John 1:12: "But as many as *received him*." It is not receiving a ritual or a church membership or communion or baptism, but a *Person*, the Son of God.

Notice too that the words *receive* and *believe* are both in the same verse. Both are interchangeable, both mean the same thing—to invite Christ to take over our lives. This is a one-time event, only once in our lives are we "born from above." "We are all the children of God by faith in Christ Jesus" (Gal. 3:26).

A man asked me after a Bible class, "I want to be born again, but just how can I receive Christ. Just what should I do?"

"If I knocked on your door when I came to visit, and you welcomed me, just what would you do?" I asked.

"Why I'd open the door and invite you to come in," he said.

"Exactly," I said. "Christ is knocking on the door of your heart, and you hear His voice by your desire to be saved. Why not invite Him to come in? He says, 'Behold, I stand at the door, and knock: if any man hear my voice, and open the door, I will come in to him.' Shall we kneel now? You ask Him to save you."

It was as simple as that. He was sincere in his desire to be born again and live for Christ; he believed that Christ was the Saviour and would take his sins away; so with his wife and son kneeling with us, he prayed and asked Christ to come into his heart.

When we rose from our knees, he said, "How glad I am to have that settled! This is my spiritual birthday!"

IV. To What Does the Water Refer in John 3:5?

The Bible always explains itself. Jesus makes it very clear that the new birth is spiritual and has nothing to do with physical things. "That which is born of the Spirit is spirit," so *water* could not refer to physical water or some ritual using water. Then what does it mean? Look up these following verses and see that one agent of the new birth is:

A. THE SPIRIT OF CHRIST, THE HOLY SPIRIT (John 7: 37-39; Gal. 3:26; Titus 3:5; John 1:12). All the promises of salvation are based on "believing in him." We are born again by receiving the Saviour, the Spirit of Christ. "Now if any man have not the Spirit of Christ, he is none of his" (Rom. 8:9). The other agent of the new birth is:

B. THE WORD OF GOD, THE TEACHINGS OF GOD'S WORD (Rom. 10:17; Eph. 5:25, 26; James 1:18; I Peter 1:23). Here the water refers to the teachings of the Word of God and never to baptism. Water never washes away sin.

V. What Is the Result of Being Born Again?

A. WE BECOME A CHILD OF GOD. "Beloved, now are we the sons of God" (I John 3:1, 2). The term *beloved* is only used for the born-again ones. The Bible does not teach the Fatherhood of God and the brotherhood of man, unless we are born again. Jesus said concerning His disciples: "Go to my brethren, and say unto them, I ascend unto my Father, and your Father; and to my God, and your God" (John 20:17).

GOD'S FAMILY

"Ye are all the children of God by faith in Christ Jesus"

Once we are born into God's family, we begin a new relationship with God. He is no longer the Judge and we the criminals; now He is our Father and we His children. Now we have the right to call upon Him in prayer; now we can know His presence to help us in trouble, "I am His and He is mine."

B. WE HAVE A NEW LIFE TO LIVE. "Therefore, if any man be in Christ, he is a new creature [creation]: old things are passed away; behold, all things are become new" (II Cor. 5:17). As a child of God we now belong to Him. Our body is the temple of the Holy Spirit who dwells in us, and we do not belong to ourselves any more. "What? Know ye not that your body is the temple of the

Holy Ghost which is in you, which ye have of God, and ye are not your own? For ye are bought with a price: therefore glorify God in your body, and in your spirit, which are God's" (I Cor. 6:19, 20). We do not belong to Satan any more, and so we do not want to follow his ways of sin. Now is the time to begin living a Christian life and obeying God's will for our lives; now we are ready for believer's baptism; we should attend and join a church, we should read the Bible and pray each day, and we can serve God.

When we become children of God we should begin to act like God's children. You know how it is when friends look at a new baby and try to find some family likeness! They think they see "Daddy's nose" or "Mother's eyes" and "Grandpa's bald head"!

Not only does God want us to be His children, but He wants us to be *good children*. "For as many as are led by the Spirit of God, they are the sons of God" (Rom. 8:14). "For whatsoever is born of God overcometh the world" (I John 5:4).

Stop a moment, and let us look at I John 3. Throughout this chapter it speaks of "doth not commit sin." In the original Greek the meaning is, "doth not practice sin," or "doth not continue to commit sin." It does not mean that we can never fall into sin, but that we do not love sin and make a practice of sin. "Whosoever abideth in him sinneth not [does not practice sin]" (I John 3:6). "Whosoever is born of God doth not commit sin [doth not practice sin]; for his seed [the Holy Spirit] remaineth in him: and he cannot sin [practice sin], because he is born of God" (I John 3:9).

One who claims to be a child of God and has no conviction of sin and continues in sin, even though he knows he is doing wrong, could not be a child of God. "He that committeth [practices] sin is of the devil" (I John 3:8).

We knew a young woman who had been reared in a Christian home, was active in church, and was known as a Christian girl. Then gradually she slipped away from church work, and then from attendance at the services, and eventually became bitter and hard. We were praying for her as a backslider to be restored to fellowship with God.

As time went on she went deeper and deeper into the sin and showed no compunction for her sin, cared nothing that her life was such a stumbling block, and had no desire to return to the church.

She became suddenly ill, and when she lay dying she told her parents, "I have never been a Christian. I tried to be religious to please you, but it meant nothing to me really. I just gave up pretending and lived my life the way I always wanted to live it. I'm not saved, and never have been, and I do not care." With these words on her lips, she died.

Too many so-called backsliders are really unsaved people and have never been born again. Parents, do not take it for granted that your children are saved just be-

cause they go along with your church activity. Make sure
that they are really born again. Unfortunately children
of God do sin sometimes; we are not perfect until we
get to Heaven. But one sign that we are the children of
God is that we do not want to sin. "My little children
[beloved born-ones], these things write I unto you, *that
ye sin not*" (I John 2:1).

However, when we sin, we do not cease to be God's
children. We cannot be "un-born"!

When our children are naughty, they do not cease to
be our children. We might wish to disown them, but
they are still ours! We discipline them if we are good
parents!

A bad child of God does not lose his salvation, but he
does lose his fellowship or friendship with God. The
bond of salvation can never be broken, but the smallest
sin breaks the thin thread of fellowship. When the fellowship is broken, we cannot see His blessing, He does
not answer prayer, His discipline and His hand are heavy
upon us (Ps. 32:4). We don't get away with anything!
The sooner we seek forgiveness and repent of our sin, the
sooner the blessing and fellowship can be restored. "If

we confess our sins, he is faithful and just to forgive us our sins, and to cleanse us from all unrighteousness" (I John 1:9).

C. WE HAVE A NEW DESTINATION. "In my Father's house are many mansions [abiding places] . . . I go to prepare a place for you" (John 14:2, 3). "The gift of God is eternal life through our Lord Jesus Christ" (Rom. 6:23). Heaven is our home; glory is our future. No one can expect to see God's home until he is born into God's family.

"Except a man be born again he cannot see the kingdom of God" (John 3:3).

Heaven will be populated with those who have received God's Son as their personal Saviour; those who have chosen to take God's way of salvation. Eternity will be occupied with enjoying the glory of God and serving Him. "His servants shall serve him: and they shall see his face" (Rev. 22:3, 4).

VI. When Should One Be Born Again?

"Behold, now is the accepted time; behold, now is the day of salvation" (II Cor. 6:2). There is no better time for a birthday than right now! Make this your birthday!

The moment you ask Christ to come into your heart, *and mean what you say*, that is your spiritual birthday.

If you have any doubt as to when you were saved, even though you have been active in the church for many years, then why not make this your day of decision and settle the matter once for all.

One gentleman dropped out of my classes, saying, "I don't follow those teachings, they aren't the same as I was brought up to believe!"

His wife begged him, "Well, go with me anyway. You don't have to believe what is taught; it's a good education at least."

He returned to the classes and came faithfully for some weeks. Then one evening they invited me to their home to answer questions and discuss the lessons. It was during that evening that we studied this subject of being born again. I remember what he said, "This is what my heart has always been wanting. How could I have rejected Christ for so long!"

"Are you willing to give your life to Him right now?" I asked.

"Yes, I am." Tears were in his eyes.

After we had prayed he called his children to him and explained that he had accepted Christ and now belonged to God. "This is my birthday into God's family."

The youngsters had been going to Sunday school and praying for their daddy. They seemed very impressed that he now belonged to God. The next day after he had gone to work the little boy said, "Mommie, if this is Daddy's birthday, don't you think we should have a birthday cake?"

"Yes, that's a good idea," said the mother, "let's make one right away!"

That night when the father came home the little boy carried the cake into the dining room. There was one candle on top. He sang, "Happy birthday, dear Daddy!"

The tears came to his father's eyes as he said, "To think how long I fought against the truth of God. How I have wasted the years!"

Why not celebrate your spiritual birthday each year? It is more important than your physical birthday, and more important than any other day in your life!

We cannot count on tomorrow. "Boast not thyself of tomorrow: for thou knowest not what a day may bring forth" (Prov. 27:1). Make today your spiritual birthday! Stop right now and ask Christ to come into your heart and then thank Him for making you His child.

One dear lady and her husband had been attending the classes; I felt they were ready to make their decision for Christ. So one afternoon I stopped to visit in their home. The wife was home alone and indeed ready for spiritual help. She asked, "How can I receive Christ?"

We prayed together. When we rose from prayer, she was smiling and crying at the same time. "Oh, I'm so happy! How can I celebrate this wonderful day?"

"Why don't you make a birthday cake and tell your family about your decision when they come home?" I suggested.

She did just that. Her husband did not say anything when she gave her testimony, but that evening the pastor dealt with him and he made his decision for Christ. They talked in the car. Then the husband went back into the house with traces of tears and a smile of peace on his face, saying, "Wife, get out that cake. It's my birthday too!"

Just where do you fit in the diagram on the next page? Are you still on the wrong side and in the wrong family? The answer for you is to receive Christ right now and know today as your spiritual birthday. Are you in God's family? Then are you a good child of God in fellowship with the heavenly Father? Has sin come into your life to break the fellowship and blessing? Now is the time to confess and forsake that sin and begin today with renewed fellowship. Whatever the need, now is the time to settle the question with God. Make this your decision day.

QUESTIONS

1. How do we know all men are not children of God?
   (I John 3:10; Rom. 9:8)

2. Why did Nicodemus need to be born from above?
   (John 3:3)

3. Why do we need to be born again? (Eph. 2:2, 3;
   John 8:44; 3:5)

4. How do we know babies go to Heaven? (Matt. 18:
   3, 10, 14; 19:14)

5. When is the sinner condemned by God? (John 3:18,
   36)

6. What is the result of being in the wrong family?
   (Rom. 1:18; II Thess. 1:9; Rev. 21:8)

7. Where will Satan spend eternity? (Rev. 20:10)

8. Are we born again by baptism? (John 1:13; Eph.
   5:25; I Peter 1:23)

9. What one act makes us a child of God? (John 1:12;
   Rev. 3:20)

10. What is the result of being born again? (II Cor. 5:
    17; Rom. 8:14)

11. Where does God dwell here on the earth? (I Cor. 6:19, 20)

12. Does a child of God want to "continue to commit sin" or "practice sin"? (I John 3:9)

13. What is God's will for His children? (I John 2:1)

14. Can a child of God ever sin? (I John 2:1; 1:9)

15. When is the best time for a spiritual birthday? (II Cor. 6:2)

16. Can we count on another time? (Prov. 27:1)

17. Can anyone get to Heaven without being born again? (John 3:3)

18. Before we are born again whom do we obey? (John 8:44)

19. What does the word *believe* mean? (John 1:12)

20. Did we deserve Christ's sacrifice on Calvary? (Rom. 5:8)

6

FAITH AND WORKS

JUST WHAT DOES THE BIBLE MEAN by faith? Even in religious circles this truth is much misunderstood, and people have some vague idea that just to believe that there is a God will make everything work out for good if you believe in yourself and in your fellow men.

How far from the truth this is! Romans 8:28 says in essence: "And we know that God works all things together for good to them that love God." To love God means more than to believe that there is a God. The demons also believe, and so does Satan himself, but they are not saved! (James 2:19).

So much of religion today is superstition; a sort of mixture of heathen fear of a great being, and a flippant idea that God is a kind old grandfather who does not care too much what we do just as long as we do the best we can!

But what does God tell us in His Word about faith?

First it speaks of *the faith*. This is the teaching of the Bible, the doctrines of God and His dealings with man (Acts 16:5; Rom. 10:8; I Tim. 4:1; 5:8; II Tim. 4:7; I Cor. 16:13; II Cor. 13:5; Eph. 4:5; Col. 1:23; Jude 3). These doctrines have not changed down through the years, and are the same today as when God inspired His apostles and prophets to write them (I Tim. 4:1). There have been no changes or additions or subtractions as far as God is concerned.

Having faith means to take God at His word. We believe that God is God, that He will keep His word and keep His promises (Heb. 11:6).

Saving faith—this topic will be discussed in this lesson.

The faithful—those who love God and obey His Word (Matt. 25:21; I Cor. 4:2; Rev. 2:10). The reward for faithfulness is blessing now and glory throughout eternity.

I. Saving Faith

God says that we are saved by faith in the Saviour. To be saved means that we are delivered from the penalty of sin which is eternal Hell, and delivered from the power of Satan's kingdom now in this present life, and some day will be delivered from the very presence of sin when we get to Heaven.

Salvation is by faith and not by works. "Therefore being justified by faith, we have peace with God through our Lord Jesus Christ" (Rom. 5:1). "Not by works of righteousness which we have done, but according to his mercy he saved us" (Titus 3:5). Nothing that we can do will take away our sin; we need a Saviour.

Salvation is the receiving of a Saviour—Someone who will take away our sin and give us a passport to Heaven. Until we receive God's way of salvation, there is nothing we can do to please Him, "all our righteousnesses are as filthy rags" (Isa. 64:6).

Suppose someone came to your home and beat your son and even killed him. Then he turned with no sense of guilt and offered to assist you in your home or business. Would you welcome such service? No doubt you would drive him away, saying, "Begone! I do not want your help!"

Yet people think they can please God by doing this or that, by going to church, keeping Lent, walking in a procession, giving money to the church, being baptized, being kind to others, but they have never received God's Son as their Saviour and are rejecting His way of salvation. Not to receive Christ is to reject Him and to be guilty of crucifying Him.

We can hardly say that we are trusting Christ when we are also trusting our own works to help save us. If we have to help God save us, then He is not God and cannot save us at all! It is not Christ *plus* our works, or Christ *plus* a church, or Christ *plus* rituals. There is only one ladder to Heaven and that is God's Son, the one way, the one door, the one Mediator, the one Lord and one faith (John 14:6; 10:9; I Tim. 2:5; Eph. 4:5).

You might say you have faith in a certain chair to hold your weight and give you rest. But if when you sit on the chair you clutch at a nearby table or another chair, obviously you do not trust the chair at all! Either Christ can save us or He cannot. He does not need our help, that is sure. "Therefore we conclude that a man is justified by faith without the deeds of the law" (Rom. 3:28; 4:5; Gal. 2:16).

II. The Steps of Saving Faith

The way of saving faith is so clearly set forth in Scripture that even a child can understand. There is no excuse for anyone to blunder and miss the way. Sad to say, men are not seeking the Bible as their guide but listen to some neighbor or some church or even to their own warped imaginations. What poor comfort to hear well-meaning friends tell the bereaved or afflicted, "Just keep your chin up! Have faith and all will be well!"

There are three steps to saving faith, and all three blend into the one act of receiving God's way of salvation.

A. BELIEVE—this does not mean that we have to know all about the Bible. But it does mean that we believe what God says about our being sinners and about Christ being the only Saviour. Faith is based upon *knowledge* of God's way of salvation. The *head* must be informed, for "faith cometh by hearing, and hearing by the word of God" (Rom. 10:17). The Bible is the only Book that gives us this truth. "How shall they believe in him of whom they have not heard?" (Rom. 10:14). Do you believe that God's Word is true? Do you believe that you are a sinner? Do you believe that Jesus Christ is the Saviour? "Believe on the Lord Jesus Christ, and thou shalt be saved" (Acts 16:31). Then you have taken the first step of salvation. Now see what the next step is.

B. REPENT—the heart as well as the head is involved in saving faith. When we see ourselves as sinners before a holy God, and *hate* that sin and want to be saved from it, then we have taken the second step of saving faith. We are to "believe in thine heart" (Rom. 1:9), and this is deeper than just a head knowledge. It includes *love* and *repentance*. "Except ye repent, ye shall all likewise perish" (Luke 13:3; Rom. 2:4; II Peter 3:9).

Salvation delivers us from *sin* as well as from Hell. "His name shall be called Jesus, for he shall save his people *from their sin*" (Matt. 1:21). There is little purpose in saying we want to be saved if we want to continue a sinful life. God does not save us to remain in sin.

There are too many people who want to be called Christians but have no desire to live a Christian life. The question is, Are they really saved?

When we are *saved*, we are saved *from* something *to* something. A man in a sinking boat, whose SOS is answered, must get out of the sinking boat and get into the rescue vessel! We are dealing with a God who knows our heart, and salvation depends on our sincerity and repentance. But sorrow for sin alone is not saving faith. Many a drunkard weeps for his plight and repents for his alcoholic spree, but he is not saved. Repentance is the second step in saving faith.

C. RECEIVE—this involves the *will*. When we realize that we are sinners, and hate our sin and want to be saved, then the next step is to *ask* Christ to save. We receive Him by praying and inviting Him to come into our heart. "If any man hear my voice, and open the door, I

will come in" (Rev. 3:20). We might not feel Him come in, for this is not a physical event, but we believe He will keep His word. We are saved by faith.

This last step of saving faith is a definite act, a one-time event, a moment of decision. It is not enough to believe *about* the Saviour, or just to be sorry for sin, we must *invite* Christ to take over our lives.

Sometimes all three steps are taken at the same time. Sometimes they come gradually. But the moment we receive Christ as our personal Saviour, that is the time of

salvation; we are born again, justified, sanctified, converted. "For whosoever shall call upon the name of the Lord shall be saved" (Rom. 10:13). "But as many as received him, to them gave he power to become the sons of God" (John 1:12). We are saved only once!

So then, saving faith includes the *head*, the *heart*, and the *will*. It is a complete surrender to Jesus Christ of all that we are and have! Even the feet are surrendered to walk for God! It is a complete "about face" from sin to God and righteousness.

HEAD
HEART
WILL
WALK

III. What Place Do Good Works Have in Saving Faith?

"For by grace are ye saved through faith; and that not of yourselves: it is the gift of God: not of works, lest any man should boast" (Eph. 2:8, 9). Works have nothing to do with salvation, *but we are saved to do good works!* "For we are his workmanship, created in Christ Jesus unto good works, which God hath before ordained that we should walk in them" (Eph. 2:10).

A new convert in the Philippines was burdened about her husband, for he was so antagonistic against the Lord and he was an inveterate gambler. Even though we managed to get him to attend tent meetings, he was not interested in becoming a Christian, and only attended because the slides and music and drawings were entertaining. Before the invitation each night, he would slip out of the tent and out of conviction's clutches. One night—and that night I slipped out—I stood behind him to block his way.

We talked long that evening, his wife and he and I, and it was that night that he prayed to ask Christ to save him. I remember thinking at the time, "My, but he has a long way to go spiritually! I wonder if he is really sincere?"

But time proved his sincerity. He really meant business with God. His gambling ceased with his other worldly habits. He came faithfully to church. He became a good friend. But there was still something bothering him, for he had not yet come out-and-out in full surrender to the Lord.

It was during our final consecration meeting at the close of the campaign, when the new converts were gathered around a huge bonfire in the empty lot beside the tent, that I watched this particular gentleman. He was very uncomfortable indeed, as one after another of the believers gave their testimony and threw into the fire things they considered hindrances to their Christian lives, much like the early Christians did in the apostles' time when they burned their books of sorcery as a testimony of beginning a new life for God. Some threw into the fire worldly literature, others threw in their cigarettes, etc., but our friend stood uneasily fumbling with something in his pocket.

Then he stepped forward. With broken voice he said, "I have been keeping something that I know I should also burn. Now I surrender it to God!" Reaching into his pocket he brought out his favorite dice and threw them into the bonfire! He had been keeping them for all those weeks "just in case" he might use them again!

Some months later he lay dying with tuberculosis. But every neighbor and former gambler friend who visited him heard the Gospel from his lips. Everyone knew that this man was really converted!

Our passport to Heaven is having Christ as our Saviour, but our reward in Heaven is for how we live for

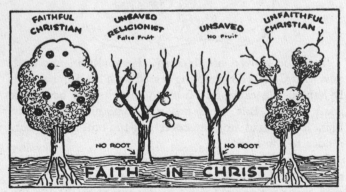

Faith is the root; works are the fruit

Him. Saving faith always produces good works. "They which have believed in God might be careful to maintain good works" (Titus 3:8).

We are justified before God by faith in Christ; we are justified before man by how we live. "Faith without works is dead" (James 2:20). "What doth it profit, my brethren, though a man *say he hath faith,* and have not works? can [*that kind of*] *faith save* him?" (James 2:14).

Saving faith *must produce fruit.* Good works are an outward sign to others that we are in Christ. "By their fruits ye shall know them" (Matt. 7:20). Faith without works is not saving faith; it is dead profession of salvation, not a real possession of the Saviour.

GOD

LOVE TO GOD

LOVE OTHERS

TO GOD

HUMANITY

The best way to serve humanity

IV. What Are Good Works in the Sight of God?

All that is done in the name of Christ and for His glory is good works in the sight of God, and brings eternal reward. "For whosoever shall give you a cup of water to drink *in my name,* because ye belong to Christ, verily I say unto you, he shall not lose his reward" (Mark 9:41). "Whosoever shall give . . . a cup of cold water only in the name of a disciple, verily I say unto you, he shall in no wise lose his reward" (Matt. 10:42).

The *motive* for our deeds determines the reward. Even the saying of prayers with the wrong motive brings only the admiration of men, not the approval of God (Matt. 6:2).

But what about civic and neighborhood welfare efforts? What about national movements like the Red Cross, orphanages, and hospitals? Are these good works?

They are good all right, but are man-to-man good works. They bring betterment here on earth by improved physical conditions, and the reward for such is here on earth, not a spiritual reward in Heaven.

That which we do because we love God and in order that others may know Him brings an eternal reward. Orphanages and hospitals that stress spiritual welfare and try to win souls to God are an investment for eternity.

The fruits of a Christian life are threefold. The tree of faith has three branches.

A. A CHRISTLIKE CHARACTER. "But the fruit of the Spirit is love, joy, peace, longsuffering, gentleness, goodness, faith, meekness, temperance" (Gal. 5:22, 23). When

we are saved, we are to be saved from sinful character traits too. There should be love instead of quarreling, joy instead of complaining, peace instead of worry, long-suffering instead of irritability. If Christ is able to save our soul, He can certainly change our disposition too! It is too easy to say, as we often hear, "I have such a hot temper that I cannot help blowing my top!" The truth of the matter is that we are enjoying our temper spells and watching everyone scamper when we are angry!

The *self* is to bear fruit when we are saved.

B. OBEDIENCE TO GOD'S COMMANDS. So many people are doing religious acts, saying many prayers, but do not really know what God's commands are for a Christian. "He that saith, I know him, and keepeth not his commandments, is a liar" (I John 2:4). The commands of the New Testament can be summarized in the following:

1. "Be ye holy; for I am holy" (I Peter 1:16). God will help us live a holy life if we are surrendered to Him. A holy life is His command for His children. It is not just a suggestion; it is a command. "Let everyone that nameth the name of Christ depart from iniquity" (II Tim. 2:19). To disobey is sin.

2. "Pray without ceasing" (I Thess. 5:17). This too is a command. To disobey is sin.

3. "Search the scriptures" (John 5:39). Time spent daily in God's Word and prayer is a must if we are to be obedient Christians. To disobey is sin.

4. "Not forsaking the assembling of ourselves together" for worship (Heb. 10:25). To gather together for worship is God's command. We don't have a choice. To disobey is sin.

5. "Ye shall be witnesses unto me" (Acts 1:8). This is God's command for each Christian. He does not give us a choice as to whether we want to witness for Him or not, but we have the privilege of witnessing by life, by baptism, and by words. To disobey is sin.

6. "Give, and it shall be given unto you" (Luke 6:38). We are to give of our time, our talents, our tithes and offerings, and our very spirits and bodies as living sacrifices unto God (Rom. 12:1; I Cor. 16:1, 2). To disobey is sin.

C. BRINGING OTHERS TO KNOW CHRIST. "I have chosen you, and ordained you, that ye should go and bring forth fruit" (John 15:16). "As my Father hath sent me, even so send I you" (John 20:21). Our fruitbearing shows itself in trying to win others for Christ. Once we know that Heaven is our home, we cannot help but want to tell others of our Lord too. It is the most natural sequence in the world. No parent is content to be saved without wanting the children to be saved; no husband is satisfied without wanting the wife to know Christ. Soulwinning is a natural result of saving faith.

To *be a Christian* depends on our faith in Christ.

To *be Christian* depends on our works for Christ.

A Christian should be Christlike. "By this shall all men know that ye are my disciples, if ye have love one to another" (John 13:35; I John 4:10, 11).

But just what does love for others mean? Certainly it does not mean that we go around seeking personal popularity. When we know that men and women are lost and on their way to Hell, real love will warn them to flee from the wrath to come. To condone and smooth over sin is not love. To pat people on the back and give them false assurance is not love. It is selfishness. We are afraid of losing our popularity. To speak the truth in love will fulfill God's command to be ambassadors for Him. *Love is a desire for, and delight in, the well-being of the one loved.*

While I was explaining the things of God to an inquirer one evening, the gentleman turned to me and asked, "If all this is true, why isn't every Christian shouting it from the housetops every day?"

I had no answer. Why? Can it be that we do not really believe that the Gospel is the power of God unto salvation? Or is it that we have no love for souls?

I remember one lady who refused to attend my Bible

classes, and shook off the invitation her neighbors gave her, by saying, "All who attend those classes become fanatics! I do not want to be a fanatic!"

Eventually, however, she got tired of making excuses, and decided to attend just once to "stop their pesterings!" That once was the beginning. She kept coming till she found Christ as her Saviour. The next thing was that she became concerned for her family and friends. Soon the neighborhood was calling her a fanatic.

To this she replied, "I'm glad to be a fanatic for Christ!"

Today this "fanatic for Christ" has seen her whole family come to Christ.

It is not love to stand by and watch our neighbors' homes burn, and not waken them "because they don't like to be disturbed." Love is to warn men and women to flee from the danger of God's judgment.

QUESTIONS

1. Does Satan believe in God? (James 2:19)
2. What is meant by "the faith"? (Jude 3)
3. What is the result of being faithful? (Rev. 2:10)

4. Do our good deeds help our salvation? (Titus 3:5)

5. What is the one way of salvation? (Rom. 5:1)

6. What is the first step of saving faith? (Rom. 10:17)

7. What is the second step of saving faith? (Luke 13:3)

8. What is the third step of saving faith? (Rom. 10:13)

9. If we are saved by faith, do we need to do good works? (Eph. 2:8-10; Titus 3:8)

10. What is the motive for good works with God? (Matt. 10:42)

11. How is our character to change when we are saved? (Gal. 5:22, 23)

12. Do we have to obey God's commands? (I John 2:4)

13. Can we be a Christian and yet not go to church? (Heb. 10:25)

14. Whom does Christ want to use to spread the Gospel? (John 20:21)

15. How can the world know we are Christians? (John 13:35)

16. Is Bible reading necessary? (John 5:39)

17. Should Christians give money to God? (I Cor. 16:2)

18. Is a man saved just because he says he has faith? (James 2:14)

19. Why does God save us? (Eph. 2:10)

20. Are we saved by faith and keeping the law? (Rom. 3:28)

7

SOULS AFTER DEATH

Curiosity about what happens after death has caused strange superstitions and speculations. Yet God has given all the information that we need about the hereafter if only men would read and believe it. Jesus Christ Himself tells what lies beyond the grave. But instead of taking what God says, people invent wild ideas of their own about reincarnation, ghosts, and hobgoblins. They completely ignore the only One who knows the answers.

Mankind is superior to other forms of life in that he is an *immortal* person. Plant life has body; animals have body and self-consciousness. Mankind has spirit, soul, and body. The soul and spirit makes up *the person*.

The body is the physical house in which the person dwells while here on earth. The soul is the self-consciousness that responds to environment and thoughts, and is the center of the senses—taste, touch, smell, hearing, sight. The spirit is that which can comprehend spiritual things; God-consciousness, conscience.

"I pray God your whole spirit and soul and body be preserved blameless unto the coming of our Lord Jesus Christ" (I Thess. 5:23; Heb. 4:12).

God created man in His own moral image in contrast to animals and plants. When the first man and woman chose to disobey God, they lost their spiritual perfection and their fellowship with God, and their physical bodies were cursed with sorrow and toil and death.

I. The Word "Death" Means Separation

When a man dies, his person leaves the body, and the body is laid in the grave and returns to dust until the resurrection. The Word of God teaches us that there is only one of two destinations for persons after death— Heaven or Hell.

II. Heaven

Heaven is an actual destination—not just a figment of the imagination, or a state to be attained here on earth.

The earth will some day be destroyed and so will the universe beyond, but God's Heaven is eternal—"a city which hath foundations, whose builder and maker is God" (Heb. 11:10). Christ said to those who loved Him: "In my Father's house are many mansions [abiding places]: if it were not so, I would have told you. I go to prepare a place for you . . . that where I am, there ye may be also" (John 14:2, 3).

III. There Are Three Heavens

A. The *first Heaven* is the atmosphere around us, where clouds are and where birds fly.

B. The *second Heaven* is the outer universe, containing the galaxies and planets outside of our atmosphere.

C. The Heaven where God abides is called the *third Heaven*. This location is also called glory, paradise, the Holy City.

God's Heaven is provided for those who have received Jesus Christ as their personal Saviour. When a believer dies physically, his body is buried to await the resurrection and is said to be "sleeping in Jesus" (I Cor. 15:16-20). The Bible does not teach "soul sleep." The persons of believers go immediately to be with Christ when they

die—"absent from the body . . . present with the Lord"
(II Cor. 5:8) ; "to depart, and to be with Christ; which
is far better" (Phil. 1:21-23) . They are in active bliss.

We are not told what the third Heaven is like, but we do
know that it well be the abode of God and His holy angels
forever, even after the end of the world when He makes a
new earth and a new universe.

Heaven is not the same as the Holy City, which will be
the center of the worship and government of the new
earth.

However, the symbolic picture we are given by John of
the Holy City, which comes down from God out of
Heaven, is a glimpse into the wealth and wonder of the
presence of the Lord to which the saved will have access
throughout eternity.

Just what do we know about the Holy City? (Read
Rev. 21:10-27; 22:1-5.) Notice that there are twelve gates.

The Holy City is as long as it is wide as it is high.
Whether it is in the form of a cube or a pyramid, it really
does not matter. Some people are worried about the size
of the city (120,000 square miles) and ask, "How can all
believers who have ever lived get into a city that size?"
Who said that we are going to live in a city? We shall
have no need for shelter or buildings throughout eternity. There will be no storms, no rain, no sun or heat;
we shall need no protection, no place to rest. Throughout eternity believers will have access to the new heavens
and the new earth and the presence of God. Like Christ,
we shall be able to go anywhere and do anything and
appear and disappear at will.

Someone else asks, "How can a pearl be large enough to be a city-gate?" That is no real problem either. Who made pearls? Cannot Almighty God make a pearl any size? And the golden streets, how can they be transparent? Gold so refined as to be used in God's Holy City could easily be transparent, if God makes it so! Whether the description of the city is literal or symbolic, it matters not; one thing we do know, and that is that it will be beautiful enough and large enough to last.

The thing that is really important is "his servants shall serve him: and they shall see his face" (Rev. 22:3, 4). We are not just going to sit on a cloud and play a harp! It will be physical and spiritual bliss, and usefulness and glory forever and ever in the presence of the Lord who loved us and gave Himself for us, and in the company of all who love Him as we do. We shall know each other and understand all things from God's viewpoint, for we shall be like Christ mentally, morally, and physically. Then we will understand why some people have to go to Hell, and we will understand why we had so many troubles here on earth, and we will understand God's plan of the ages and *the mysteries of the universe*. You then can visit Mars without a space suit if you want to!

IV. There Are Two Main Resurrections

A. THE FIRST IS FOR BELIEVERS. "Blessed and holy is he that hath part in the first resurrection: on such the second death hath no power, but they shall be priests of God and of Christ, and shall reign with him a thousand years" (Rev. 20:6). The first resurrection takes place when Christ returns to take believers to glory with Him.

Until the resurrection of believers, those who die in the Lord now are only in spiritual bliss in Heaven because their bodies are in the grave. At the resurrection they receive bodies which will be like Christ's resurrection body. Remember, when Christ rose from the dead He was recognizable and could eat, speak, had flesh and bones. But He was different in that He could pass through closed doors; He could appear and disappear from sight; He could go up into the clouds; gravity had no power over Him. "When he shall appear, we shall be like him; for we shall see him as he is" (I John 3:2). We will never hunger, never suffer, never die. Hallelujah! "So also is the resurrection of the dead. It is sown [buried] in corruption; it is raised in incorruption . . . it is sown [buried] a natural body; it is raised a spiritual body" (I Cor. 15:42-44). So throughout eternity believers will be in physical and spiritual bliss.

"But I would not have you to be ignorant, brethren, concerning them which are asleep. . . . Them also which sleep in Jesus will God bring with him. . . . For the Lord himself shall descend from heaven with a shout . . . and the dead in Christ shall rise first" (I Thess. 4:13-16).

B. The Second Resurrection Will Be for Unbelievers. "I saw the dead, small and great, stand before God; and the books were opened. . . . And the sea gave

"The dead in Christ shall rise first"

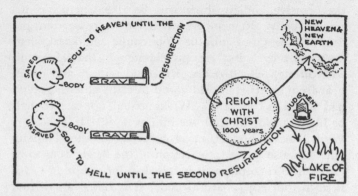

up the dead which were in it; and death and hell delivered up the dead which were in them. . . . And death
and hell were cast into the lake of fire. This is the second
death. And whosoever was not found written in the book
of life was cast into the lake of fire" (Rev. 20:12-15).

V. Hell

The Bible teaches more about Hell than it does about
Heaven. Hell is a location. It is not here on earth, nor
is it a thing of the imagination. Hell is a place of spir-

itual torment in this age because the bodies of the unbelieving dead are in the grave. Hell is believed to be in the center of the earth. "The way of life is above to the wise, that he may depart from hell beneath" (Prov. 15:24).

Unbelievers are not annihilated after death—they do not cease to exist. They exist in a condition of ruin and conscious separation from God throughout eternity. "The Lord Jesus shall be revealed from heaven with his mighty angels, in flaming fire taking vengeance on them that

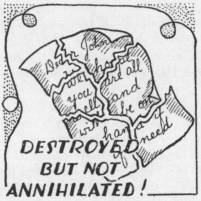

DESTROYED BUT NOT ANNIHILATED!

know not God, and that obey not the gospel of our Lord Jesus Christ: who shall be punished with everlasting destruction from the presence of the Lord, and from the glory of his power" (II Thess. 1:7-9). The word *destruction* does not mean annihilation. You can destroy a piece of paper, but it is not annihilated. Though it is burned and the ashes scattered, the chemical formula still remains. There is no annihilation of *anything*, including men. To *destroy* means to "cease from its original capacity; to be ruined."

"The fire that never shall be quenched: where their worm dieth not, and the fire is not quenched" (Mark 9:

43, 44) . Here the word *worm* is an old English expression referring to the "germ of life," or the soul. Everlasting destruction is everlasting separation from God in torment.

The question is asked, "But does fire really mean literal fire in connection with Hell?" The Bible often uses the word *fire* simply as being symbolic of some trial or suffering or testing, etc. However, whenever God's Word is symbolic it usually gives the explanation. In the case of Hell fire, it is never explained to be anything other than literal fire. "It is better for thee to enter into life halt or maimed, rather than having two hands or two feet to be cast into everlasting fire" (Matt. 18:8) .

Someone else asks the question, "If God is a God of love, how can He create anything so cruel as an eternal Hell?"

Hell was not made for men. It was made for Satan and his angels. But men who disobey God and follow Satan will have to go with the Devil some day. God is a God of love, and for that reason He provided a Saviour for sinners. Those who reject God's Son and trample under foot the blood of the Son of God cannot hope to escape eternal punishment and they deserve it.

VI. The Lake of Fire

There is a difference between Hell in this age and the lake of fire throughout eternity. Those in Hell now are in spiritual torment only, for their bodies are in the grave. After the second resurrection the bodies of unbelievers will be raised and become spiritual bodies which cannot die or be destroyed. Throughout eternity they will be in physical and spiritual torment in the lake of fire. The Bible does not say just where the lake of fire will be, but of one thing we are sure, it will not be in the center of the earth, for God makes a *new earth* "wherein dwelleth righteousness" (II Peter 3:13).

But there is no doubt about there being a lake of fire. "And the devil that deceived them was cast into the lake of fire and brimstone . . . and shall be tormented day and night forever and ever. . . . And death and hell were cast into the lake of fire. This is the second death. . . . The lake which burneth with fire and brimstone: which is the second death" (Rev. 20:10, 14; 21:8).

Such verses as these take the frivolity out of the subject of Hell. How many people laugh and say, "I don't care if I go to Hell; there'll be plenty of company there!" There will be plenty of others there, yes. But company, no! There shall be weeping and gnashing of teeth. It is not good company when everyone is gnashing his teeth. There is no love in Hell, no peace, no hope, no light, no mercy, no friendship; no such words as *mother, sweetheart;* not even one drop of water! Hell is no laughing matter.

A woman with whom I was pleading to accept Christ as her Saviour, said, "My husband died without knowing religion. If he is in Hell then I don't want to be saved. I want to be with him!" Poor comfort for her, for neither she nor her husband would love each other in Hell.

One man said, "I can't afford to become a Christian, for I'd have to give up my business!"

"What is your business?" he was asked.

"I sell liquor."

"Well, just how much money do you expect to make the rest of your life?"

He figured for awhile and then came up with a handsome sum in hundreds of thousands.

"Would you take a check right now for that amount, and know that you will spend eternity in Hell?"

He hesitated and thought for a moment, then finally

shook his head. "No, I guess not. That's too cheap a price for my soul!" That day he accepted Christ as his Saviour, and changed his business!

"What shall it profit a man if he gain the whole world, and lose his own soul?" (Mark 8:36).

VII. Destinations of the Old Testament Dead

Now we come to a different phase of teaching. (Read Luke 16:19-31.) In the Old Testament times people did not go to Heaven to be with Christ—Christ had not come to earth yet. They went into the "abode of the souls of the dead" called Sheol (Hebrew), Hades (Greek), or

BEFORE THE DEATH OF CHRIST

PARADISE
(BLISS)

A GREAT GULF
FIXED

TORMENT

Destinations of the souls of dead

Hell in the center of the earth. It had two compartments. The righteous went into paradise, and the wicked into torment or Gehenna. Paradise was also called "Abraham's bosom" and was a place of spiritual bliss. Torment was spiritual torment. Between the two compartments was a void or gulf that could not be crossed. This emptiness is not purgatory or limbo or any intermediate state, but a vacuum or invisible barrier so that those in paradise could not pass to the place of suffering and those in the place of suffering could not pass to the place of comfort.

Both places were in Hell, the abode of the souls of the dead.

Read over the story Christ tells of the rich man and Lazarus who died. This is not merely a parable, for Jesus

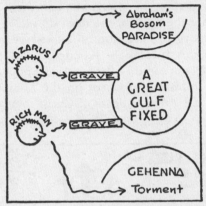

gives the name of the beggar and He does not give names to fictitious characters. Both the rich man and beggar died; one was taken into bliss and the other into torment. Both are very much awake and conscious. Souls do not sleep.

Someone asks, "If their bodies are in the grave, how could they be in bliss or torment?"

Remember, the soul is the center of the senses, the self-consciousness. They were very much alert.

When the rich man wanted Lazarus to come to help him, he was told that there is no passing back and forth. The great gulf is *fixed*. The dead do not change their destination after death; there is no second chance after death.

Then suddenly the rich man seems to have a missionary vision! But he gets it too late (Luke 16:27-31). A few moments in Hell proves there is a Hell. If those who are living on earth could have but one glimpse of Hell, per-

haps we would all be missionaries. If Christians really believed that unsaved people are really lost, and that Hell
is eternal, everyone would be in full-time soul-winning!

But just as those in torment are never without their
suffering, and those in bliss never lose their joy, so it is
also true that the souls of the dead do not return to the
earth in this age. There are no ghosts! A very few exceptions to this rule might be cited in Old Testament
days. Samuel appeared to the witch of Endor, and Moses
and Elijah appeared to Christ on the Mount of Trans-
figuration, and after the death of Christ some of the dead

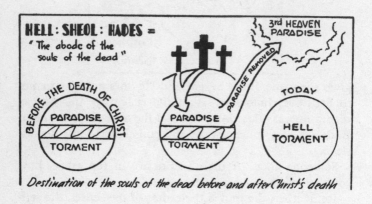

Destination of the souls of the dead before and after Christ's death

appeared in Jeursalem. But such were extreme cases—
exceptions.

When Christ died, He went into paradise. Remember,
He said to the thief on the cross, "Today shalt thou be
with me in paradise" (Luke 23:43). Paradise was in the
center of the earth in the place called Sheol, Hades, Hell.
Christ went down into Hell while His body was in the
tomb. "His soul was not left in hell, neither his flesh did
see corruption" (Acts 2:25-31). Christ died, really died.

His body was laid in the tomb and His spirit went into the bowels of the earth. "He also descended first into the lower parts of the earth" (Eph. 4:9, 10).

When Christ rose from the dead and ascended up to Heaven, He took the godly souls from paradise with Him: "When he ascended up on high, he led captivity captive, and gave gifts unto men" (Eph. 4:8).

Now paradise is in Heaven where Christ is. Hell today stands only for torment.

How do we know that paradise is now in Heaven? In II Corinthians 12:1-4 the apostle Paul tells of his own experience when he was stoned to death and was caught up into the third Heaven. He calls this third Heaven "paradise." So paradise today is in the third Heaven where Christ is.

If in the Old Testament times it was impossible to pass from paradise to suffering or vice versa, and yet the two places were in the same location, *how much greater the impossibility* for souls to pass from Hell to Heaven in these times! Heaven and Hell are more than countless universes apart! And yet the wonder of it all is that the moment we leave the body in death, we are present with the Lord. Time and space mean nothing to God!

VIII. Is it Possible to Contact the Souls of the Dead?

Since the souls of the dead do not hover over their bodies after death, and since they depart immediately to either Heaven or Hell, and since they do not change their destination or return to the earth, and since we have no Scriptural assurance that they can communicate with us or we with them, therefore it is indeed impossible to contact the dead.

But what about those who claim that they have contact with the dead? The increase in the cults of so-called spiritualism is a sign of the last days, and the delving into the occult and mysticism of the spirit world is certainly becoming more and more popular. Are they all fakes? By no means. But they do not contact the dead. Then whom do they contact?

There is indeed a spirit world around us. God is Spirit and the Holy Spirit is here in the earth today. The angels of God are around those who fear Him. Satan is a spirit and is going to and fro through the earth. Satan's helpers, the demons, are around us with the intention of keeping men from God and tempting those who belong to God.

God warns against those who traffic in spiritism. "All that do these things are an abomination unto the Lord" (Deut. 18:10-12). God commanded spiritists to be stoned to death. In Revelation 21:8 we are told that they shall have their part in the lake of fire. So certainly God is not co-operating with those who contact spirits. This is true too of God's angels who serve Him. The souls of the dead do not return to the earth. In the process of elimination, only Satan and his demons are left! Spiritism is really demonism.

The Bible teaches about "familiar spirits," or demons, who are assigned by Satan to become familiar with the habits, manner of life, voice, etc., of human beings and to tempt them. When a medium lays her mind open to spirit control, the familiar spirit takes over (Isa. 8:19, 20). This demon can answer questions about the life of the dead for he is familiar with them, and Satan will do anything to dupe people into seeking his advice.

There are many fake mediums who trick the public with rigged-up tables and séance rooms, but there are also the genuine mediums who do contact spirits, evil spirits.

There is a tendency in these modern days for men to scorn the teachings of the Bible about demonism. However, Jesus speaks of demon possession and He is not referring to insanity or neurosis either. Missionaries from the foreign fields have many a brush with satanic manifestations, and have seen demons cast out of tortured souls who come for help.

Even here in America there are many incidents of demon possession. A young lady told me of her experience in spiritism. She was brought up among those who practiced the occult, and soon found out that she had the gift of being able to go into a trance and of being used by the spirits. Soon she was "preaching" at their spiritist meetings, and would go into a trance and give her sermon without having any idea of what she said. In time, friends told her what she preached, and she was amazed to find she was quoting Scripture verses that she had never even read. She had no Bible. This intrigued her so greatly that she bought a Bible and looked up the verses.

Then the trouble began. She saw that she was not preaching the truth of what the verses said!

Being of an honest turn of mind, she tried to quit the cult and her part in the meetings, but she was too deeply involved to get out easily. Pressure was brought to bear upon her by her friends and leaders. But worst of all, Satan did not want to lose a disciple and used every wile to keep her in his clutches. She was molested by voices and spirit manifestations, and for awhile she thought that she would lose her mind.

But God is stronger than Satan, and His Word gradually began to bring deliverance. For some years she floundered in horrible confusion, and then she met those who could lead her to Christ. What a wonderful Saviour is Jesus my Lord! It was only then that she found peace of mind and heart, and peace from the spirit world as well.

As you read this, do you feel a little nervous?

You do not have to be!

Before we receive Jesus Christ as our personal Saviour, we are all children of the Devil, and the deeds of our father we will do (John 8:44). We think his thoughts and obey him and will go with him to Hell some day.

But *when we accept Christ,* the Holy Spirit dwells in our hearts, and Satan's power is broken. "Greater is he that is in you, than he that is in the world" (I John 4:4). We do not need to fear Satan and his demons when God is on our side! To make it even more wonderful, "the angel of the Lord encampeth round about them that fear him, and delivereth them" (Ps. 34:7). What power can Satan have when we are in the hollow of God's hand! We are "kept by the power of God" (I Peter 1:3-7).

Satan can do nothing without God's permission!

QUESTIONS

1. How is mankind different from other forms of animal life? (I Thess. 5:23)

2. How do we know Heaven is not here on earth? (John 14:2)

3. When does a believer go to Heaven? (II Cor. 5:6, 8)

4. Where is Hell now? (Prov. 15:24)

5. What will believers do in Heaven? (Rev. 22:3, 4)

6. When will be the first resurrection? (I Thess. 4: 13-17)

7. How long will souls suffer in the lake of fire? (Mark 9:43, 44; Rev. 20:10)

8. Where was paradise in the Old Testament? (Luke 16:22)

9. Do the souls of the dead change destinations after death? (Luke 16:26)

10. Where did Christ go while His body was in the tomb? (Acts 2:25-31; Luke 23:43)

11. When did the Old Testament saints go to Heaven? (Eph. 4:8)

12. Where is paradise now? (II Cor. 12:1-4)

13. Does God approve of spiritualism? (Deut. 18:10-12)

14. Is it possible for spiritist mediums to contact spirits? (Isa. 8:19, 20)

15. How do we know that the story of the rich man and Lazarus is not a parable? (Luke 16:20)

16. What kind of a body will the resurrection body be? (I Cor. 15:44)

17. What will be the final destination of spiritists? (Rev. 21:8)

18. Who is said to be "asleeping in Jesus"? (I Cor. 15:18; I Thess. 4:13, 14)

19. Do souls sleep after death? (Luke 16:23)

20. Will the lake of fire be in the center of the new earth? (II Peter 3:13)

8

PRAYER

THE SAYING OF PRAYERS is one of the most-practiced religious rites of all nations and ages. In human hearts there seems to be an inherent longing for help from some higher being. From the jungles to the mountains and the islands of the sea come the voices of prayer in many languages. The sad part of the story is that so few know what almighty God says about prayer, and the rite has come to be little more than a superstitious formula to ward off evil or bring aid.

While traveling in China, we met a tiny old lady climbing the steep steps up the mountainside leading to a heathen temple. She stopped to wipe her brow in weariness and pain as we spoke to her, for she was climbing the worn stone steps on her knees.

"Old lady, where are you going?"

"I go to the temple to pray and find peace of heart," she answered discouraged.

"Why do you climb on your knees? The path is long and hard."

"Oh, I have been there so many times before and found only emptiness of heart. This time perchance the gods will smile on me, for I come in greater humility!"

In the Philippines I questioned a woman who spent long hours in devout prayers.

"What is your burden of heart that you pray so often and so long?"

"I must repeat these prayers so many times because I

failed to donate to the church a share of the price of the sale of my pig last week. I say these prayers for penance."

In California a man told me, "Every night I say a prayer before I go to sleep in case something will happen to me during the night."

In the Chicago area a young couple insisted they were Christians, "because all our prayers are answered. Everything we pray for comes to us. We are the luckiest couple alive. God must be with us!"

But just what does God say about prayer?

Prayer is not just getting something or avoiding something or atoning for something or easing our conscience. Prayer is the highest privilege of mankind to commune with God. We speak to Him and He speaks to us. It is like a two-way telephone line to glory. Too often we think of prayer as merely a one-way line where we can talk and talk, or ask and ask, and do not care or wait to listen to what God has to say to us. We rush through a long list of requests and then rush away without waiting to know what God expects from us. There is nothing more frustrating than to talk on a one-way telephone and have no assurance that there is anyone listening at the other end. Or to have to listen and listen and have no way of saying a word in return!

Did you ever realize that when we pray we are showing our love for God and bringing joy to His heart? "Now I beseech you, brethren, *for the Lord Jesus Christ's sake,* and for the love of the Spirit, that ye strive together with me in your prayers" (Rom. 15:30).

Before we can know answers from God and before we can even reach His throne of grace, we must know what He says about prayer.

I. To Whom Should We Pray?

In order to be sure that God will hear us, we must take His Word as the guide. Too many people are saying prayers without the faintest idea of what God says on the subject, and then are surprised and disappointed when they do not receive their answers.

A. WE ARE COMMANDED TO PRAY TO GOD IN HEAVEN (Matt. 6:9; I Cor. 1:2; Acts 12:5). In these verses we are told to pray to God the Father and God the Son. There is no indication in the Bible that anyone except God can hear our prayers. We are to "come boldly unto the throne of grace, that we may obtain mercy, and find grace to help in time of need" (Heb. 4:16).

Suppose we let the telephone represent prayer as the means of directly reaching God. Someone might ask the question, "But would it not be to our advantage to pray to others in Heaven too, just to be sure the requests reach God? Since saints in glory are so close to God, do they not have some influence with Him? What about the apostles or Mary? Could we not pray to them to pray for us because there is advantage in praying one for another?"

True, God says that we should pray one for another (James 5:16). But the problem of praying to the saints in Heaven is that we have no scriptural assurance that they can even hear our prayers. If Mary and Peter were here on earth, it would indeed be a joy to share our burdens with them and have a prayer meeting with them; in fact, the last we hear of Mary in the Bible she was in a prayer meeting (Acts 1:14). But no one was praying *to her.*

Since the saints in Heaven are not deified, and since we are told to pray directly to God, we insult Him when

Whosoever shall do the will of my Father which is in heaven, the same is my brother, and sister, and mother.

we try to come to Him in some roundabout way. It shows our lack of faith in Him, and that is sin.

But do not those in Heaven have more influence with God than we do? Surely Mary must be more accessible and has more power with Christ than we do!

Well, let us see what Christ says. In Matthew 12:46-50, we have the statement of Christ Himself regarding His human relatives: "Whosoever shall do the will of my Father which is in heaven, the same is my brother, and sister, and mother."

Then look in John 2:4, 5. Here Mary tries to suggest to Christ what He should do and He does not remedy the situation immediately. She does not take offense for she realizes that He is right, and her power over Him as her Son is over: He is now taking His place as the Son of God. She then gives her only command, "Whatsoever he saith unto you, do it" (John 2:5).

In other words, even when Christ was here on earth Mary was not closer to Him or had more influence with Him than those who obeyed Him. The same holds true today. Those who do the will of God are as close to Him and have as much influence with Him as anyone in Heaven. After all, if Christ lives in my heart, how much closer could I be to Him!

Well, if I pray to God, does it matter if I pray to the saints too, just to make sure? Disobeying God will not "make sure" of answered prayer. It is sin. You know and I know that the shortest distance between two points is a straight line. So the shortest and surest way to God is directly *to Him,* and not in some roundabout way that disobeys Him. Take the Bible alone as the guide for answered prayer.

B. WE ARE COMMANDED TO PRAY IN THE NAME OF JESUS CHRIST (John 14:13, 14; 15:16; 16:23; I Cor. 1:2). But what does it mean to pray in Jesus' name? Does it mean that we must close each prayer with those very words? It is good to close our prayers by saying, "We ask this in Jesus' name," but that is by no means the meaning of this phrase.

Suppose you went to a bank where you had no account and tried to cash a check for $1,000.00. The teller would look at the record, at the signature and then at you and shake his head. "I'm sorry, but you have no account here!"

This did indeed happen to me in a strange city. I needed cash to pay for my auto repair, but no one would cash my check. Eventually one bank manager asked, "Do you know anyone in this town who does have an account with us?" I remembered a pastor in whose church I had spoken some weeks before. They called him, and he co-endorsed my check. As soon as he had signed, I got the money!

When we come to the bank of Heaven we need Someone to sign our check! We have no account there! God does not answer because I come in *my name* and ask for *my glory*. However, if Christ will endorse the request, it means that He approves, and I shall receive the answer. You see, He has an account in the bank of Heaven.

Our prayer-telephone has a telephone post that upholds the wire that carries our message to the throne in Heaven. Let us represent this by the "one mediator between God and men, the man Christ Jesus: "who gave himself a ransom for all" (I Tim. 2:5, 6). It is because of His sacrifice on Calvary that we have a Mediator who ever lives to intercede for us (Heb. 7:25). This Mediator is not "the woman, Virgin Mary," or "the man, Peter," for only Christ died for our sins.

We are commanded to pray in the name of Jesus and no other. We have no need of others to plead our cause. He is *in us* and *with us* and *for us* if we have received Him as our Saviour. We can't get closer to Him than that!

C. WE ARE COMMANDED TO PRAY WITH THE HELP OF THE HOLY SPIRIT (Rom. 8:26, 27). "The Spirit also helpeth our infirmities: for we know not what we should pray for as we ought: but the Spirit itself [himself] maketh intercession for us . . . he maketh intercession for the saints according to the will of God." It does not say, "He maketh intercession *to the saints!*" We are to "pray in the Spirit" (Eph. 6:18).

Now, before we receive Christ as our Saviour, we belong to our father the Devil. We have no access to God. But when we receive Christ as our Saviour, the Holy Spirit comes into our hearts and we belong to God. In other words, when Christians pray, God the Father and God the Son and God the Holy Spirit all work with us and for us! No wonder prayer is so important! It is the most wonderful privilege in the world!

II. Who May Pray?

We have almost answered this already. In Luke 18: 10-14 we have the story of two men who went to pray. Both were sinners, although one of them did not think he was. One admitted his sin and confessed it, and was justified. The other prayed *with himself;* his prayer never reached God at all.

There is only one prayer that God will hear from the sinner, and that is, "God, be merciful to me a sinner." When we utter that prayer in sincerity, God takes our sin away and we belong to Him. This is true of the unsaved as well as of Christians. "If I regard iniquity in my heart, the Lord will not hear me" (Ps. 66:18). This does not say, "If I acutally sin." But just to condone sin, not to rebuke it deep in our hearts, cuts off our prayer power. God knows our thoughts afar off!

The unsaved cannot pray except for forgiveness and salvation.

Oh, but right away someone argues, "I know God has answered my prayers, even though I haven't been, as you call it, 'saved.' I've always gotten what I wanted!"

The Bible gives the answer to that. The rain falls on the just and the unjust. God allows good to come to the wicked as well as to the good. "The goodness of God leadeth thee to repentance" (Rom. 2:4). God allows good things to come to the unsaved that they might turn to God in gratefulness. Unsaved folk may get what they want, but it is *not in answer to prayer.* God says it is not. It is simply circumstances. With the Christian there is no such thing as *luck* or *chance;* everything is *Providence.* "All things work together for good to them that love God" (Rom. 8:28).

But there is still the second phase to this question of who may pray.

The telephone service to Heaven is connected when we accept Christ as our Saviour. But sometimes the line gets out of order! There is one thing that will hinder our prayers from reaching the ear of God—*sin*.

We have a dear friend who is a telephone man as well as a glowing Christian. One day while trouble-shooting a rural line, he could find nothing wrong with the wires no matter how hard he searched, and was about to return to the office to report when he happened to look up and saw a sort of thin string hanging high between two wires. Stopping his truck, he climbed the pole, and found that some youngsters had been playing with a dead snake, and had flung it up high into the air where it had crossed the wires. The snake was short-circuiting the wires.

Our friend in typical manner moralized, "Is that not just like our enemy, that old serpent, the Devil! He causes us to sin and then our telephone line of prayer is short-circuited!"

That is why the unsaved cannot pray, and that is why the Christian with unconfessed sin in his life cannot pray. The phone is out of order!

The unsaved and the backslider have one thing in common—their prayers will not be answered. "Your iniquities have separated between you and your God, and your sins have hid his face from you, that he will not hear" (Isa. 59:2) .

SHORT CIRCUIT !

III. Hindrances to Prayer

Sin comes in many forms.

A. UNBELIEF HINDERS ANSWERS TO PRAYER. "Without faith it is impossible to please him: for he that cometh to God must believe that he is, and that he is a rewarder of them that diligently seek him" (Heb. 11:6) . Nothing is impossible with God. We cannot expect God to answer our prayer when we do not really believe that He is almighty God or that He can answer. God will always answer prayer that reaches His ear; sometimes the answer is "yes"; sometimes, "not now"; sometimes, "something better"; but there will be an answer. Too many times we come with our request but deep down we really do not believe God can do it. Have you ever prayed, "Lord, save my husband . . . but he's hopeless, Lord!" We limit God by our unbelief. God says: "But let him ask in faith, nothing wavering . . . for let not that man think that he shall receive anything of the Lord" (James 1:6, 7). To waver in prayer means to be undecided, doubtful, unbelieving, not sure of what we want.

I remember vividly an occasion in the Philippines when my husband was away on a trip and I was left in charge of the evangelistic campaign in a very antagonistic town. A sudden typhoon blew up and threatened to flood the location where our Gospel tent was standing. The unsympathetic people of town knowingly wagged their heads and said, "Whenever we have a typhoon the river overflows, and the place where your tent stands is six feet under water!"

Could God stop a typhoon? I had never heard of a typhoon to end in less than four to seven days. I prayed hurriedly, but with an eye on the rising river, and my mind full of plans and fears; I knew the typhoon could not die away.

Calling the Christians, we got busy and batted down the tent, piled the equipment up high on the benches, tightened the ropes, and added more stakes. As we toiled in frenzied haste, the riverlets of water began to seep over the river bank, and the rain came down in sheets while the wind blew in terrific gusts.

When all was done that I could think to do, we gathered for a prayer meeting. Is that not like us human beings! We call upon God as a last resort instead of trusting Him first! As we prayed, I kept wondering, "Can God stop a typhoon?" Mentally I knew He *could*, but *would* He?

At first I felt no faith in prayer. Then I stopped wondering, and prayed, "Lord, this is Thy work, and Thy testimony, and Thy equipment. Undertake, Lord. Have Thy will. Thou art able!"

In the earnestness of prayer I forgot the rain, the impending flood, the tent canvas slapping and straining at its ropes in the gale.

Then we all stopped and listened in amazement. The wind had dropped. The rain had stopped drumming on the canvas. We looked out to see the low clouds breaking overhead and blue sky peeping out! The storm had ceased! There was no more rain; the river settled back into its bed.

How hard we had to work to unpack all the equipment and set up the benches again for the meeting that night! Served us right!

B. A WRONG MOTIVE HINDERS PRAYER. "Ye ask, and receive not, because ye ask amiss, that ye may consume it upon your lusts" (James 4:3). We come demanding something from God regardless of whether it is His will or not. We do not want His best for us; we want our own will, as a child might cry in willfulness to play with a knife. Sometimes God answers such prayers with discipline. We "cut our fingers!" "And he gave them their request; but sent leanness into their soul" (Ps. 106:15).

How much better, when we pray, to come with a desire for God's will! "And this is the confidence that we have in him, that, if we ask anything according to his will, he heareth us" (I John 5:14). Instead of telling God what to do, we will avoid frustration when we lay the matter before Him and trust Him to work out the right answer.

A mother had a little son she loved dearly. He was a beautiful child, and she was greatly distraught when he became very ill. Much prayer was offered for the lad, but the mother prayed with fierce demanding, "Lord, let him live! Don't take him from me!"

God answered that prayer. The boy lived. But for several years he lay helpless in his bed unable to sit up, to speak, or to feed himself.

He became ill again. This time her prayer was different, "Lord, have Thy will! If you want to take our boy to Heaven it's all right." God took the child to be with Him.

"Commit thy way unto the Lord; trust also in him; and he shall bring it to pass" (Ps. 37:5).

C. NOT READING AND OBEYING GOD'S WORD HINDERS PRAYER. "He that turneth away his ear from hearing the law, even his prayer shall be abomination" (Prov. 28:9). The law refers to God's Word and His will. How many people are saying prayers and are not reading the Bible! Unless we are spending time with God's Book each day and obeying what He tells us, our prayers are not pleasing to God. They are repulsive to Him—an abomination!

A young man came to me in great consternation. "I have lost my faith in prayer! I prayed and prayed that my mother would not die, and she did die!"

I knew the chap quite well and knew that he had been far from following the Lord for some years, so there was only one answer I could give him: "John, it is not a matter of God not being able to answer prayer, but He could not answer you if you have been out of fellowship with Him."

On another occasion a father was pleading with God to spare his child.

"It seems that Heaven is brass over my head!" he cried. "God does not hear me!"

"Is there any reason why He should not hear you?" I asked.

"Well," he hung his head. "It has been a long time since I went to church or read by Bible, and I've neglected prayer, and I guess I'm a backslider."

"Then you will have to start praying for yourself before you can pray for Danny."

That day the prodigal son returned to his Father, and God heard his prayer. His little boy was restored.

D. EMPTY REPETITION OF WORDS HINDERS PRAYER. "The effectual fervent prayer of a righteous man availeth much" (James 5:16). "What things soever ye desire, when ye pray" (Mark 11:24). It is the earnestness and motive of prayer that brings answers, and not the many words. Effectual prayer never repeats empty words. "But when ye pray, use not vain repetitions, as the heathen do: for they think that they shall be heard for their much speaking" (Matt. 6:7).

Vain repetition means reciting of words. Any words that we say without really thinking or meaning what we say is vain repetition.

In Tibet they have solved their prayer problems in a practical way. They have one prayer, and that is the name of Buddha, "Thou Jewel of the Lotus." They repeat this over and over again, and think they will gain merit by the number of times it is repeated. To simplify the matter, they write the name on wheels which they turn by hand or place in waterfalls which say the prayer for them when they are busy! They even put the name of Buddha on flags which the wind will "pray" for them! For a little cash they can even hire someone to turn their prayer wheel for them!

You say, how ridiculous! And yet people in America are doing just about as foolishly by repeating prayers that mean nothing to them. Our heavenly Father treasures heart conversation with His children, and not some memorized or repeated words that someone else has written.

To repeat God's name, or anyone else's name, over and over again, or the same request over and over, gains no merit with God. Earnest prayer is prayer with a desire. Pray what is in your heart. Pray just as you talk to a loving father or a friend.

Even Christians make vain repetitions when prayer is said unthinkingly. Even spontaneous prayer can be empty repeating of words if we are not thinking what we are saying. Grace asked at the table can be empty words unless we think what we say. God does not listen to mere form or ritual. The very best-phrased prayers at prayer meeting can mean nothing to God if we are wondering more about what people are thinking than of what God is thinking.

During prayer meeting one night in a small country church, the people were much impressed by the very well-phrased, eloquent prayer of a visitor. After the meeting a kind member shook hands with the visiting gentleman and said, "I surely did appreciate your wonderful prayer tonight." But she was surprised at his answer.

"Oh, that's nothing! You should hear me when I'm in practice!"

E. DISHARMONY IN THE CHRISTIAN HOME HINDERS PRAYER. "Likewise, ye husbands, dwell with them [wives] according to knowledge, giving honor unto the wife, as unto the weaker vessel, and as being heirs together of the grace of life; that your prayers be not hindered" (I Peter 3:7). Christian homes should be harmony homes. Quarreling and bickering hinders prayer; we are to live "gracefully" together. It is true that in homes where only one member is a Christian it is hard always to keep peace. There the Christian must be sure that the friction is not his fault, and he will have to live all the godlier so as to win the unsaved one. How much we all need God's help in these days so that our home life be consistent before our loved ones and children! No one can afford to live a prayerless life.

F. AN UNFORGIVING SPIRIT HINDERS PRAYER. "And when ye stand praying, forgive, if ye have ought against any. . . . But if ye do not forgive, neither will your Father which is in heaven forgive your trespasses" (Mark 11: 25, 26). An unforgiving spirit is sin. We cannot very well expect God to forgive us our sin if we want to keep it, can we? Also if we know someone has a grudge against us, we should make it right with him, and then come to worship and serve God (Matt. 5:23, 24).

IV. Prayerlessness Is Sin

Christians are commanded to pray. "Pray without ceasing" (I Thess. 5:17). "Men ought always to pray, and not to faint" (Luke 18:1). This is a command, and not just a mild suggestion. The prophet Samuel said: "God forbid that I should sin against the Lord in ceasing to pray for you" (I Sam. 12:23). Not to pray is sin. How much blessing and help Christians forfeit because they do not lay hold of the wonderful power of God released through prayer! "Ye have not, because ye ask not" (James 4:2). Are we living in this sin of prayerlessness? Do we gather as a family around the Word of God each day? Do we take time for reading and prayer alone with God each day? Are we faithful in the prayer meeting? Why not? Do we not believe in prayer?

V. Should Christians Pray the Lord's Prayer?

The prayer in Matthew 6:9-13 is really a sample prayer that Jesus gave to His disciples. The Lord's prayer is in John 17. We never find anyone in Scripture repeating prayers; the prayer in Matthew 6 is a pattern. It was given primarily for the Jewish followers of Christ, and its reference to the kingdom is to the kingdom of Christ when He will be the King on the earth and Israel will once again be the chosen people in fulfillment of the promises given Abraham. Of course, Christians may pray this prayer if they realize and really mean what they are saying. But if this is not the prayer of our hearts, there is no earthly good in saying it. Certainly there is no advantage in repeating it over and over. We shall not be heard for our much speaking.

And yet in churches all over the world congregations are repeating these words again and again, sometimes for merit, for ritual, or for penance, or just plain superstition, and never understand what it really does mean.

Let us analyze it.

A. "OUR FATHER WHICH ART IN HEAVEN." To begin with, God is not our Father until we are born into His family by faith in Christ. So if we have never been born from above, we are wasting our time. Vain repetition!

B. "HALLOWED BE THY NAME." This means, "All holiness be unto thy name." But how can anyone offer holiness to God's name when our own lives are not holy? Unless we are living in fellowship and holiness with God we are saying empty words.

C. "THY KINGDOM COME." The kingdom of Christ is the Kingdom Age when Christ will rule the earth. One thing will hasten this day and that is the winning of souls. When the last soul is saved that God has ordained to be saved, then Christ will come. If we are not doing a thing to win souls, these words are vain repetition!

D. "THY WILL BE DONE ON EARTH, AS IT IS IN HEAVEN." We cannot pray this honestly unless we are doing God's will in our own lives.

E. "GIVE US THIS DAY OUR DAILY BREAD." Well, now at last this is a safe request! Everyone needs food! But the Word of God says: "Man shall not live by bread alone, but by every word that proceedeth out of the mouth of God." So here too there is a spiritual meaning. When we neglect the Word of God, we cannot pray this prayer!

F. "AND FORGIVE US OUR DEBTS, AS WE FORGIVE OUR DEBTORS." An unforgiving spirit is sin, so God cannot forgive us as long as we want to keep our sin.

G. "AND LEAD US NOT INTO TEMPTATION, BUT DELIVER US FROM EVIL." Many times we do not even go round the block to avoid temptation, and yet we ask God to do a private miracle and keep us from temptation and "deliver us from evil." We can often answer our own prayer by surrendering to the will of God, and there is no use praying these things if we do not really want to do His will.

H. "FOR THINE IS THE KINGDOM, AND THE POWER, AND THE GLORY, FOREVER. AMEN." To ascribe glory to God forever must begin right here on earth by our living for His glory in whatsoever we do (I Cor. 10:31). There is no use praying that He will have glory throughout eternity when we are not living for His glory right here! Vain repetition!

Yes, Christians may pray this prayer, but be sure we mean what we say; otherwise we are making vain repetitions like the heathen do.

How wonderful it is that God so often does answer our prayer even though we are so unworthy! The goodness of God is too great for us to fully comprehend.

A Christian lady was much burdened for her unsaved husband. We were all praying for him, but he seemed so hard and indifferent and so addicted to his liquor. I remember the day she searched my face and asked, "Do you think God will answer prayer for him?"

"Do you think He can?" I asked.

"Yes, I suppose so," she sounded hesitant, "but how do I know it will be God's will to save my husband?"

"Your problem is not to know if God will save him or not; your business is to pray in faith believing that God *can* save if it is His will, and leave the rest to Him."

In the weeks that followed opportunities opened to present the way of salvation to that husband, but even though he listened politely enough, he showed no desire to believe.

One night he turned to his wife, and asked, "Are you one of those 'saved people'?"

THE THRONE OF GRACE

WHEN WE CAN'T REACH LOST SOULS ON OUR FEET, WE CAN ALWAYS REACH THEM

ON OUR KNEES

Timidly she said, "Yes, I am."

He grunted, "I thought so."

He left the house shortly afterward to go down to the liquor store to return his empty bottles and restock his supply, as was his weekly habit.

In her own words the lady told me what happened. "When he came home, he had no bottles of beer. Instead he had a can of tomato juice under his arm! Do you think now that God is going to answer our prayers and save him?"

I had to smile. "It is still for God and your husband to say as to whether he will be saved or not. But it is for us to keep praying and witnessing."

The next time I went to visit in the home and invited the husband to attend my Bible classes, he said he would come. He did come, and kept coming.

Some weeks later I stopped him after the evening service and asked him, "Just when are you going to receive Jesus Christ as your personal Saviour? You have quit drinking, true, but you are not saved until you receive the Saviour."

"I know," he replied, "but I want to make my life better before I say I'll become a Christian."

"Do you think you can do a better job of cleaning up your life than Christ can?" I asked. "After all, that is what He wants to do for you."

That evening while his wife and Christian friends gathered around, he surrendered his life to Christ who alone can make our lives acceptable unto God. He came "just as he was," sin and all.

That was the beginning of only two years of witnessing for his Lord before he went to glory. But none of his fellow workers or companions could say they had not heard the way of salvation; they heard it from this living witness who was himself an answer to prayer.

God *can* answer prayer. Why not give Him a chance?

QUESTIONS

1. For whose sake do we pray? (Rom. 15:30)
2. To whom should we pray? (Matt. 6:9; I Cor. 1:2)
3. Do we need to hesitate to come to God? (Heb. 4:16)
4. Does Mary have more influence with God than we do? (Matt. 12:50)
5. What is Mary's one command? (John 2:5)
6. Who is our Mediator in prayer? (John 14:13, 14; I Tim. 2:5)
7. Who helps us pray? (Rom. 8:26, 27)
8. Can the unsaved receive answers to prayer for material things? (Ps. 66:18)
9. Does everything work out for good for everyone? (Rom. 8:28)
10. What will short-circuit our prayer? (Isa. 59:1, 2)
11. Will God answer undecided, unbelieving prayer? (James 1:6, 7)
12. If we ask, will we always receive? (James 4:3)
13. Can we pray even though we don't take time to read the Bible? (Prov. 28:9)
14. Does repeating of prayers help bring answers? (Matt. 6:7)
15. What two requirements are given in James 5:16 for prayer to be answered?
16. Can Christians have their prayers answered even though they do not get along in the home? (I Peter 3:7)
17. Is it any of our business if someone has a grudge against us if we do not hold a grudge against him? (Matt. 5:23, 24)
18. What is one of the main reasons we do not receive more answers to prayer? (James 4:2)
19. Who may pray the Lord's Prayer? (Matt. 6:9)
20. Do we have a choice of either praying or not praying? (Luke 18:1)

9

SANCTIFICATION

THIS WORD *sanctify* is not as mystical or difficult as some seem to think. It simply means "to be set apart."

The primary Bible meaning of the word is "to set apart from Satan and sin unto God."

In the Old Testament God on the earth dwelt in the tabernacle and temple, and they were said to be "sanctified unto the Lord." "For now have I chosen and sanctified this house, that my name may be there" (II Chron. 7: 16).

But in and since New Testament days, God dwells in the hearts of believers. "The most High dwelleth not in temples made with hands" (Acts 7:48). "Ye are the temple of God" (I Cor. 3:16).

I. Why Do We Need To Be Sanctified?

Because all of mankind are sinners and as sinners sold out to the Devil, we are "set apart" unto sin. If we are to see God and dwell with Him forever, we must belong to Him by being "set apart" for God. Until we are saved, Satan dwells in us—we are his temple. When we are saved, God dwells in us, and we become His temple, sanctified and holy.

II. When Is a Person Sanctified?

Sanctification may be viewed as *past, present and future; or instant, continuous and complete.*

A. INSTANT SANCTIFICATION—SAVED FROM THE PENALTY OF SIN

"Ye are washed, but ye are sanctified, but ye are justified in the name of the Lord Jesus, and by the Spirit of our God" (I Cor. 6:11).

The very moment a person receives Christ as his Saviour, he is washed from his sins; he is justified before God; he is sanctified; he is born into the family of God.

The moment we are sanctified, we step over the line from *lost to saved.* We are saved from the penalty of sin—eternal Hell.

Every saved person is a sanctified person, a saint. Saints are not canonized after they have died. Every sinner becomes a saint the moment he is sanctified, saved. If he is not a saint on earth, he will never get to Heaven at all! "Unto the church of God . . . to them that are sanctified in Christ Jesus, called to be saints" (I Cor. 1:2). The Bible speaks of the saints on earth, and none were perfect people. They were saved people (Eph. 1:1; 6:18; Phil. 1:1). They were children of God.

B. Continuous Sanctification—Saved from the Power of Sin

"For this is the will of God, even your sanctification, that ye should abstain from fornication" (I Thess. 4:3). "But grow in grace, and in the knowledge of our Lord and Saviour Jesus Christ" (II Peter 3:18).

The secret of growing in grace is to grow in knowledge of the Lord Jesus. To know more about Him is to want to be more like Him.

The moment we have stepped into the family of God, we are set apart for Him, and we are to grow more and more like Him. We do not grow *into* sanctification, but we grow *in* sanctification. We don't become saints by trying to be good, but we want to be good *because* we are saints. "We . . . beholding as in a glass the glory of the Lord, are changed into the same image from glory to glory, even as by the Spirit of the Lord" (II Cor. 3:18).

The secret of increasing from glory to glory is to behold the glory of the Lord. In other words, when we take time to study His Word and pray and learn of Him, we want to become more and more like Him. We become saints by receiving the Saviour, but we become saintly by living for Him. God not only saves us from the penalty of sin; He is able to save us from the power of sin, the old serpent, the Devil himself. "And the Lord make you to increase and abound in love one toward another, and toward all men . . . to the end he may stablish your hearts unblamable [not sinless] in holiness" (I Thess. 3:12, 13). "As ye have received of us how ye ought to walk and to please God, so ye would abound more and more" (I Thess. 4:1).

There is such a thing as "perfecting holiness" or becoming mature in holiness. The word *perfect* in the Greek means "mature," not sinlessness. "Let us cleanse ourselves from all filthiness of the flesh and spirit, perfecting holiness in the fear of God" (II Cor. 7:1).

This does not refer to sinless perfection on earth in this life. Saints of God do not want to sin, but sometimes they fall into sin. The proof that they are saved is that they confess and forsake sin and want to be holy (I John 1:8, 10; Rom. 7:15-25).

Someone asks, Then what is meant by some who teach the "second blessing," or that the "second work of grace" is a spiritual emotional experience that sanctifies? They believe that after being saved, one is not sanctified until one has this experience of tarrying and praying and emotionalizing, and then he is sinless and holy, and the ability to sin is removed.

The apostle Paul does not teach such a doctrine. He made many return visits to his converts to give them another blessing and to establish them in the faith, but it had nothing to do with sinless perfection. Every visit he made to them was another blessing.

Among those who teach this doctrine it is common to hear, "Be saved and sanctified!" But God's Word teaches that to be saved *is to be sanctified!* God does encourage and command us to grow in sanctification.

While riding on a bus, I overheard two Negro ladies talking behind me. They were discussing favorably a new acquaintance, and one was saying, "She sho' am a good woman!"

"Is dat right?" exclaimed the other. "Is she a Christian?"

"Oh, yes," said the first, "she sho' loves de Lord."

"Really!" The second woman was interested. "Is she sanctified?"

"Oh, lan's sakes, no! She am a Baptist!"

It was all I could do to keep a straight face and keep out of their conversation!

III. Problem of Sin

Why do we have such a problem with sin while we are here on the earth? Everyone has a self-nature called in the Bible, the "old man." This old nature is self-will against God. When we are saved and sanctified, we have a new nature born in us, a spiritual nature, called the "new man" (Eph. 4:18, 22-24; John 8:44; Rom. 8:7-9; Gal. 5:16-26; Rom. 6:13; 8:6; John 3:3; I Cor. 5:17).

As long as we are unsaved there is no spiritual life, and the old nature is in full control under Satan. We serve sin and love sin. *But* when the new nature is born, then the problem begins! Now there are two natures, and they are in variance with each other!

The Christian life is called a warfare. "For the flesh lusteth against the Spirit, and the Spirit against the flesh: and these are contrary the one to the other: so that ye cannot do the things that ye would" (Gal. 5:17; Rom. 7:15-25). The apostle Paul knew the meaning of this battle within his heart, and exclaimed in despair, "O wretched man that I am! Who shall deliver me from the body of this death?"

But the battle isn't hopeless. Victory is available *if we want it*. The apostle ends his despair with hope, "I thank God through Jesus Christ our Lord!" "But thanks be to God, which giveth us the victory through our Lord Jesus Christ" (I Cor. 15:57).

The fact of the matter is, too often we really do not want victory; we enjoy our sin and relax our guard, and the old nature walks all over us. But the normal Christian life is the victorious life. It is the only life that will glorify God. "Let everyone that nameth the name of Christ depart from iniquity" (II Tim. 2:19-21).

An old Indian, who had newly found Christ as his Saviour, expressed the problem in this way: "In my heart there are two dogs that are continually in battle, a white dog and a black dog."

The missionary asked him, "Which dog wins the battle?"

The answer was simple, "The one that I feed!" He certainly was right. Just what are we feeding upon spiritually? Are we eating up the things of the world, the movies, TV, radio, etc.? Or are we feeding on the living Bread, the milk of the Word, the meat of God's teachings? Are we wondering why we have no victory and yet we prefer worldly friends to Christians and the dance floor perhaps to the house of God?

IV. How Can We Be Sure of Victory?

This is a practical everyday experience, moment by moment kept by the power of God, because *we want to be kept.* See what Romans 6 has to offer on this subject.

A. KNOW that we are new creatures in Christ; that we belong to God; that Christ can give us victory. "Knowing this, that our old man is crucified with him . . . that henceforth we should not serve sin. . . . Knowing that Christ being raised from the dead dieth no more" (Rom. 6:6, 9).

I am crucified with Christ...

Christ liveth in me
GAL 2:20

Realizing that we are saved, and that Christ can give victory from the power of sin, are the first steps in victory.

B. RECKON that the new self is alive to God and the old self is counted dead. "Reckon ye also yourselves to be dead indeed unto sin, but alive unto God through Jesus Christ our Lord" (Rom. 6:11). Every moment *remember* that the Holy Spirit lives in us, and we have been bought with a price. Count the old nature dead! Do not respond to the whisperings of sin and temptation. After all, God expects us to co-operate with Him in the

Christ liveth in me

matter of victory over sin. "He that is begotten of God keepeth himself, and that wicked one toucheth him not" (I John 5:18). God keeps us from sin *if we want to be kept.*

C. YIELD to God daily, hourly, and moment by moment. Send up an SOS of prayer when temptation comes. We have constant and instant contact with God when we need victory. "Neither yield ye your members as instruments of unrighteousness unto sin, but yield yourselves unto God ... your members servants to righteousness unto holiness" (Rom. 6:13, 19).

V. Complete Sanctification—Saved from the Presence of Sin

This will be when we get to Heaven. "To the end he may stablish your hearts unblamable in holiness before God, even our Father, at the coming of our Lord Jesus Christ with all his saints" (I Thess. 3:13). "And the very God of peace sanctify you wholly; and I pray God your whole spirit and soul and body be preserved blameless unto the coming of our Lord Jesus Christ" (I Thess. 5:23).

When we see Christ, we shall be like Him; we shall be saved from the very presence of sin. The old nature will be taken away, and we shall be perfect, sinless, and completely holy. Remember this when you look at other Christians. Some day we will be perfect. In the meantime let us be patient with each other and love one another in spite of imperfections. Keep our eyes on Christ as our example, and not on people. None is perfect here.

"Beloved, now are we the sons of God, and it doth not yet appear what we shall be: but we know that when he shall appear, we shall be like him; for we shall see him as he is. And every man that hath this hope in him purifieth himself, even as he is pure" (I John 3:2, 3).

VI. How Can a Christian Be Sure of Pleasing God?

There is a sure test as to what is right or wrong for a Christian, and this test will guarantee blessing and success before God. There is no real joy when we do not do God's will and commands.

So if we desire real *joy*, here is the threefold test:

A. "Whether therefore ye eat, or drink, or whatsoever

ye do, do all to the glory of God" (I Cor. 10:31) . Everything we do—that includes our social life, our pleasures, our habits, our business. If we cannot ask God's blessing on what we do, and know it is glorifying to Him, then *it is sin.*

> Can our pleasures pass this 3-fold test?
>
> **Jesus**   DO ALL TO THE GLORY OF GOD
>
> **Others**   THAT THEY MIGHT BE SAVED
>
> **You**   WILL LIVE A LIFE OF THANKS-LIVING

B. "Not seeking mine own profit, but the profit of many, that they might be saved" (I Cor. 10:33) . Every thing we do and say, even our language, our homelife, our manner of dress—should not hinder others from wanting our Lord. If what we do or say will hinder others from being saved, then *it is sin.*

C. "And whatsoever ye do in word or deed, do all in the name of the Lord Jesus, giving thanks to God and the Father by him" (Col. 3:17) . Everything we do—our thoughts, our ambitions, our entertainment—should be done in the name of Christ and in order that we shall live a life of thanksgiving. Thanksgiving means thanks-living too! If what we do or think hinders us from loving Christ, or takes away our appetite for the prayer meeting or serving God, and our life is not a thanks-living unto God, then *it is sin.*

As Christians and saints, everything we do, say or think

should pass the threefold test. If there is any doubt, be sure it is wrong! If we cannot pass the test, it is sin for a sanctified child of God and grieves the Holy Spirit. We do not have to get our ideas from other people—God has given us His answer on any doubtful question about practice or pleasure if we just use His test.

Are you saved? Are you born again; are you a saint of God?

Then are you growing in sanctification? Are you becoming daily holier and more and more victorious?

If not, why not?

A young policeman in the Philippines had come to know Christ as his Saviour, and his testimony had made quite an impression on the almost 100 per cent unsaved town. But he came to me with his problem one day, saying, "I know I am saved, but I just cannot overcome my habit of smoking!"

"Why do you want to break the habit?" I asked.

"Because I know I cannot glorify God with it, and I know it is harmful to my body. It has become such a habit, for I have smoked since I was a boy, and now I see I am a slave to tobacco."

"You are right," I told him, "it is wrong. But the God who can save you from Hell can certainly save you from sin. Do you not believe that?"

Together we prayed about the matter, and yet he seemed to have no victory. Time after time he came back to admit his failure and ask prayer. I spent many hours with that young man, but he never seemed to overcome his habit.

"Juan," I said to him one day, "unless you cut off this last tie to sin, you will be dragged back into sin and into the world. You will never find success in the Christian life."

"Oh, no," he vowed, "I'll never go back into the world!"

Those words still echoed in my mind after we had left that town and gone on to other evangelistic campaigns, and I could not cease to pray for Juan.

But news of him was heartbreaking. He gradually dropped out of church, and from the fellowship of the believers. Soon he would not even speak to them in the street. Then he married a girl of another faith. The whole town was sneering at the small Baptist church when such a promising convert seemed to turn back to his old life. That is one of the main problems when a Christian backslides; it does so much damage to the testimony and name of Christ! No one backslides alone; we always harm others.

The pastor and Christians could never get near that young man to talk with him. Then he became ill, very ill. But even then, when they tried to visit him, the wife would guard the door and refuse them entrance.

It was one day when the wife was at the market that the Christians slipped in and gathered around Juan's bedside. The tears came to his eyes, and he begged them, "Oh, please sing to me the hymns that we used to sing in the meetings when the Friederichsens were here. How my heart has hungered for those days!" As they sang, Juan wept. Then he begged, "Please pray for me! How I want to come back to my Lord!"

They told me his words after his restoration. "Just to think that it was all because I would not break loose that one last tie to sin that Satan dragged me back into backsliding. What a price I have paid! And how I have hurt my Lord! I surely pray that I may be taken to Heaven before I will ever want to backslide again."

Juan really meant business with God this time. He let his wife know his decision, and the Christians came regularly to visit him until he recovered.

It was the week he first got out of bed that we came back to that town for a conference. He was eagerly planning to attend. On the way to the church, however, a sudden cloudburst soaked him and gave him a chill, and he had to return home instead. I never saw Juan again.

A week later he went to be with the Lord. God had heard his desire, rather to go to glory than to backslide again; everyone who knew him knew of the change in his life. He made his wife promise before he died that he should have the Baptist pastor perform a Christian funeral.

That was the first Christian funeral in that town. Yes, Juan had a real testimony in his death, and the message rang out to heathen ears for the first time as they crowded the cemetery in curiosity. But even though his death had been a real witness for God, just think what his life might have been! His triumphant funeral service could never blot out the year of backsliding and sin, nor make up for the testimony and service for God he might have seen. No, it does not pay to live in sin. It does not pay to keep even one last tie to the world.

Can your life pass the threefold test?

In contrast to Juan there was a young woman who was engaged to a very promising and well-to-do doctor. She was a Christian, but he was not. It was during the reviving of the power of God in the church where I happened to be speaking that that young woman realized that God commands that Christians should only marry "in the Lord" and not be "unequally yoked together with unbelievers." She could not pass the threefold test with her engagement. I will always remember the day that she stood with tears streaming down her face and prayed that God would give her strength to give up her fiancé unless he would come to God for salvation.

That young man did not come to God. She kept her word, though, and she broke her engagement. That heartbreaking experience was a triumph to that young woman. Her life was that much stronger; her testimony was that much more powerful. God gave her a Christian husband some time later!

QUESTIONS

1. Where did God dwell on the earth in the Old Testament days? (II Chron. 7:16)
2. Where does God dwell on the earth today? (I Cor. 3:16)
3. When is a person sanctified? (I Cor. 6:11)
4. Who are the saints? (I Cor. 1:2; Eph. 1:1)
5. What is God's will for Christians? (I Thess. 4:3)
6. What is continuous sanctification? (I Thess. 3:12, 13)
7. What is the "old man"? (Eph. 4:18-22)
8. Why does a Christian have conflict in his heart? (Gal. 5:17; Rom. 7:15-25)
9. Is victory available? (I Cor. 15:57)
10. What must we *know* in order to have victory over sin? (Rom. 6:6, 9)
11. What must we *reckon* in order to have victory over sin? (Rom. 6:11)
12. What are we to *yield* unto God? (Rom. 6:13, 19)
13. When will we be completely sanctified? (I Thess. 3:13; I John 3:2)
14. What is the threefold test? (I Cor. 10:31, 33; Col. 3:17)
15. How does a Christian grow in sanctification? (II Peter 3:18)
16. What is the "new man"? (Eph. 4:24)
17. What must Christians depart from? (II Tim. 2:19)
18. Is tobacco, gambling, or the theater mentioned in the Bible? (I Cor. 10:31)
19. How do we become more and more like Christ? (II Cor. 3:18)
20. What is the result of being "in Christ"? (II Cor. 5:17)

10

ETERNAL LIFE

WHAT DOES THE BIBLE MEAN by "eternal life"? It is more than just a condition of life. It is a Person! It is to be acquainted with that Person!

"This is life eternal, that they might know thee the only true God, and Jesus Christ, whom thou hast sent" (John 17:3).

Jesus Christ said: "I am the way, the truth, and the life: no man cometh unto the Father, but by me" (John 14:6). Eternal life is Christ Himself. He is the source of physical and eternal life; He alone can give eternal life.

"These are written, that ye might believe that Jesus is the Christ, the Son of God; and that believing ye might have life through his name" (John 20:31). To believe in Christ means that we receive eternal life.

In other words, eternal life is Christ, and for me to have eternal life is to receive Christ. Eternal life is to have Christ in my heart and to live with Him throughout all eternity! It is an everlasting union with Christ.

We give over our human life to Him and He gives us spiritual life. He lives in us to save us, and we live for Him to please Him. It is a union of faith and love that nothing can break asunder.

"Who shall separate us from the love of Christ? . . . For I am persuaded that neither death, nor life, nor angels, nor principalities, nor powers, nor things present, nor things to come, nor height, nor depth, nor any other creature [created being], shall be able to separate us from the love of God, which is in Christ Jesus our Lord" (Rom. 8:35-39). Nothing and no one, not even Satan or even we ourselves, can separate us from Christ once we have received Him as our personal Saviour. His love is everlasting love.

What is the difference between eternal life and everlasting life? Both are spoken of in the Bible. *Eternal life* is the spiritual life that Christ gives, for He is eternal. *Everlasting life* is life that shall never end. When I receive Christ, He is eternal, but His life begins in me when I am saved, and it is without end, so is everlasting with me. Both terms are used interchangeably in Scripture.

I. When May I Receive Eternal Life?

The moment I receive Jesus Christ as my Saviour, I have eternal life. "He that believeth on the Son *hath* everlasting life" (John 3:36). "He that hath the Son hath life; and he that hath not the Son of God hath not life" (I John 5:12). How much clearer can the Bible be! When Jesus said, "I am the truth," He meant that we can

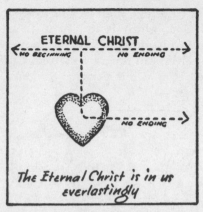

The Eternal Christ is in us everlastingly

know the truth about God from the Word He has given. The words of the writings of the apostle Paul *are the words of Christ!* Paul received them from the ascended Lord.

Jesus also said, "I am the way." He is the way to Heaven; He is the Saviour to save us from sin and Hell. He also said, "I am the life." Because of Him, we have life forever in Heaven. Everlasting death is everlasting separation from God in the lake of fire.

II. How Can We Know That We Have Eternal Life?

A. GOD SAYS WE CAN KNOW. If we say we cannot know for sure that we are saved, we call God a liar. "These things have I written unto you that believe on the name of the Son of God; that *ye may know* that ye have eternal life" (I John 5:13). Look up these other promises too, where God says that we *have* (present tense) eternal life when we receive Him: John 3:14-16, 36; 5:24; 10:9, 27-29; 6:47. We are saved by faith, and faith is believing God will keep His word. He does the saving, we do the receiving!

B. THE WORD "ETERNAL" MEANS WITHOUT END. If we can lose our everlasting life, it is not everlasting! A wedding ring is supposed to be a symbol of everlasting love. Unfortunately, human love does end sometimes, but God's love never ends! If we lose our eternal life when we sin, it means that our salvation depends upon our being good! But God's Word says we are saved by receiving a Saviour, and not by being good (Titus 3:5). If we have to help God save us, then He cannot save at all; He is not God! Eternal life is a *Gift*. "The gift of God is eternal life" (Rom. 6:23). We receive the Gift, and live a life of thanksgiving!

C. SAVED MEANS "SAVED"—not maybe, or perhaps, or if you hold out till the end! Once we are born into God's family, we cannot be un-born! If we in God's family are lost again when we sin, just how many sins does it take to lose salvation? Only one? If so, each time we sin we must be saved again; and after we are saved, we should be baptized again! The Bible says that we should believe and be baptized! So every time we are angry or jealous, or irritable, or lie, or are selfish, we must be saved again, and then baptized again—and again—and again! How contrary to the Word of God! *Saved* is in the passive tense; it is something done for us. We have been saved by the Saviour. "Whosoever shall call upon the name of the Lord shall be saved" (Rom. 10:13).

D. THE HOLY SPIRIT SEALS THE BELIEVER. "And grieve not the holy Spirit of God, whereby ye are sealed unto the day of redemption" (Eph. 4:30; 1:13, 14). God will not break His seal; God cannot lie. "He which hath begun a good work in you will perform it until the day of Jesus

Christ" (Phil. 1:6). "Kept by the power of God through faith unto salvation" (I Peter 1:5). We take the Saviour, and then He takes us!

You board a bus for the city. First, unless you board it you will just stay put. Once you board the bus, you relax and let the bus take you. Some people think that after they take "salvation" they have to push it all the way to the destination! God's "bus" never breaks down!

E. THE CHARACTER OF GOD ASSURES ETERNAL LIFE. "Who hath saved us, and called us . . . not according to our works, but according to his own purpose and grace. . . . I know whom I have believed, and am persuaded that he is able to keep that which I have committed unto him against that day" (II Tim. 1:9-12). "In hope of eternal life, which God, that cannot lie, promised before the world began" (Titus 1:2).

Jesus said, "I give unto them eternal life; and they shall never perish, neither shall any man pluck them out of my hand" (John 10:28). The word *man* is not in the original text. No demon, no human being, can pluck us out of His hand! "My Father . . . is greater than all; and no[ne] is able to pluck out of my Father's hand. I and Father are one" (John 10:29,30).

NO NEED TO PUSH!

Too often our feelings are influenced by our environment or our health or happenings, but our salvation is based upon a Saviour who is able to keep. "For I know whom I have believed, and am persuaded that he is able to keep that which I have committed unto him against that day" (II Tim. 1:12).

III. Is Everyone Who Says He Is a Christian Sure of Heaven?

We cannot know the hearts of others; that is God's knowledge. But we can see the fruit of eternal life in a saved person. There are so many "professions" of salvation, but too few real "possessions" of the Saviour. Many think they are saved because they raised their hands, or went forward in a service, or because they joined a church or were baptized or confirmed, or had some emotional experience. But salvation is the definite *act* of receiving Christ and being willing to be saved from sin and from Hell. This is a one-time event, a new birth, and we immediately begin to live a new life.

"SAVE ME, LORD,— BUT DON'T MAKE ME GIVE UP SIN—!"

We cannot fool God. To ask for salvation and want to keep our sin is hypocrisy. There is no salvation or eternal life when we come to God "with reservations" or with fingers crossed, saying, "Lord save me, but I want to keep my sin!" Insincerity nullifies prayer for salvation. A change of living accompanies the receiving of eternal life. Too often "they profess that they know God; but in works they deny him" (Titus 1:16).

IV. Who Is a Backslider?

A. DEFINITION. A backslider is a Christian who has slipped out of fellowship with God. A Christian does not love sin. Even though he may fall into sin, he does not remain out of fellowship with God, but confesses his sin, forsakes it, and finds mercy. The fellowship is then restored (I John 1:7, 9).

Many times people are called backsliders when they have never been saved. After all, you cannot slide back until you have been forward!

The Bible gives a very apt definition of a backslider: "The backslider in heart shall be filled with his own ways" (Prov. 14:14). The moment a Christian turns to his own way instead of God's ways, he is a backslider.

But, someone asks, "Just because a person is saved,

does that mean that he can sin without restraint?" God says: "What shall we say then? Shall we continue in sin, that grace may abound? God forbid. How shall we, that are dead to sin, live any longer therein?" (Rom. 6:1, 2).

A saved person does not want to sin. He has a new nature that is born of God and he hates sin and loves righteousness. "Whosoever is born of God doth not continue to practice sin." Consider for illustration the animal kingdom. Now the pig loves the mud, rolls in the mud, and will go right back to it again even if he is scrubbed up and dressed in pink ribbon! It is his nature! On the other hand, sheep or cats do not like mud. They avoid it. It is their nature! Oh, yes, a cat may fall into the mud; a sheep may slip into the mire—but they do not

lie down and roll in it, they hate it and get out and dry themselves off as quickly as possible. That is the difference.

The same is true of saved and unsaved persons. The unsaved love sin and their own way—care nothing for the will of God. The saved hate sin and love righteousness and seek the will of God for their lives. They may fall into sin, but they do not remain in sin; they do not *practice* sin, but confess and forsake it, and find mercy.

But do not think for one moment that a Christian who backslides will "get away" with sin. God does not send His children to Hell, but He does discipline them. He will not overlook sin. "Whatsoever a man soweth, that shall he also reap" (Gal. 6:7). God will use His big stick *"Trouble"* to spank His wayward children.

GOD'S BIG STICK!

B. THERE ARE FIVE RESULTS OF SIN IN THE LIFE OF A CHRISTIAN:

1. *God will not answer prayer.* "If I regard iniquity in my heart, the Lord will not hear me" (Ps. 66:18).

2. *God will allow trouble* and sorrow, sickness, and even physical death. "For this cause many are weak and sickly among you, and many sleep" (I Cor. 11:30). "There is a sin unto death: I do not say that he shall pray for it" (I John 5:16). The "sin unto death" is when a Christian is such a poor testimony that God removes him from the earth. So often we think that when a Christian dies, he has gone to his reward and his work on earth is done. Not always! Sometimes he has simply been taken away before he does any more damage! Does this come as

a shock to you? It should. It is a serious warning of how important it is not to be a poor testimony (I Cor. 5:5).

3. *We hinder others* from being saved. There are more people hindered from coming to God because of the life of some Christian than any other reason. Instead of being the salt of the earth and the light of the world, to make people thirsty for God and show them the way, the backslider is a stumbling block. "When ye sin so against the brethren, and wound their weak conscience, ye sin against Christ" (I Cor. 8:12).

4. *We lose our reward* when we get to Heaven. "If any man's work shall be burned [destroyed by God's testing], he shall suffer loss" (I Cor. 3:15). "And now, little children [new Christians] abide in him; that, when he shall appear, we may have confidence, and not be ashamed before him at his coming" (I John 2:28).

5. *We grieve the heart of God* our Father. "Grieve not the holy Spirit of God" (Eph. 4:30). What is more heartbreaking than a child who does not love his father or mother!

My parents were missionaries in China for thirty years. Because they lived far inland where there were no schools, each of us children had to go to boarding school a month's journey away. One by one, as we grew old enough, we were left at school, and my parents had to return to their work with empty, broken hearts. My oldest brother was just a little boy when he first went away. Patting mother's face, he whispered, "Don't let your face change, Mother!" Being missionaries, our parents did not have the fare or the time for travel, and we were all teenagers when we met them again. As a youngster of fifteen, I can remember how embarrassed I was when my mother kissed and hugged me. I had not been hugged in all those years! It took some months before I felt at ease with my parents, and I often wonder if my mother's heart did not break many times a day as she yearned for us to love her as she loved us.

Another missionary friend did not win back the love of her children. Her daughter continued to resent her, and the early love was never restored.

But there is no reason why we should be strangers to God. He has not left us; He never fails. Yet sometimes we call ourselves children of God and are breaking His heart because we do not love Him; we do not have the same interest in His work; we do not love His Word; we do not hunger for prayer; we do not care for holy things.

V. What Is the Result of Having Eternal Life?

Anyone who has a one-sided view of this subject of eternal life will now get the other side! Yes, there are two sides to every doctrine. They balance perfectly. These results of eternal life are the outward sign that we are saved. "By their fruits ye shall know them."

IF ANY MAN BE IN CHRIST.

old things are passing away...

SIN

A. WE SHOULD WALK IN NEWNESS OF LIFE. The indwelling Christ will give us power to live a new life. "Therefore if any man be in Christ, he is a new creature [creation]: old things are passed away; behold, all things

are become new" (II Cor. 5:17; Rom. 6:4, 13; Col. 3:1-4).
"Old things are passing away" is the literal meaning in
the above verse. Sinful things should be dropping off
daily and constantly as we grow in grace. You know,
some species of oak trees keep their old, dead leaves all
through the winter. How can they be removed? Pick
them off, shake them off? No, just wait until the spring
when the new sap seeps up through the tree and reaches
the branches, and new buds begin to form. Then the old,

dead leaves fall off! With the new life of Christ stirring
in our hearts, old things of sin and things that are ques-
tionable will begin to drop off. If they do not glorify God,
they do not appeal to us either.

B. WE SHOULD WALK IN THE LIGHT OF RIGHTEOUSNESS.
"He that followeth me shall not walk in darkness, but
shall have the *light of life*" (John 8:12). Light refers
to righteousness. Christ saves us from the power of sin
and makes victory over sin possible. When we keep close
to Him, we become more righteous. The farther we go
from Him, the more self-content and self-righteous we
become. You know how it is at banquets and fancy din-
ners, when candlelight is used. Even the most wrinkled

face looks fairly beautiful! Perhaps that is why women like candlelight! The electric light by contrast is revealing!

God's holiness is pretty revealing too. The saved person desires to follow Him closely and walk in the light every day.

C. WE HAVE THE WATER OF LIFE, AND THE BREAD OF LIFE. Christ is able to satisfy the hunger and thirst of the soul. He satisfies the longing heart. "Blessed are they which do hunger and thirst after righteousness: for they

shall be filled" (Matt. 5:6). If Christians are hungering for the things of the world, it is because they are not coming constantly to Jesus and feasting on Him spiritually. He says: "I am the bread of life: he that cometh to me shall never hunger; and he that believeth on me shall never thirst" (John 6:35).

D. WE HAVE ABUNDANT LIFE. The Christian life should not be a mere existence, but a full, active, happy living. Rich living is Christian living! God's presence and blessing come now, and Heaven for all eternity! Jesus said: "I am come that they might have life, and that they might have it more abundantly" (John 10:10). God's will is for us to be strong, healthy, and productive in this life. Those of us who try to raise plants or flowers know that what we want is a plant that is strong and healthy and bearing flowers. But sometimes the plant is alive, yes, but barely alive! Sickly and sad and fruitless, we are ashamed for it to be seen! God wants us to have abundant life, radiant and glowing for Him.

E. WE SHOULD LOVE THE SOULS OF OTHERS. "Holding forth the word of life" (Phil. 2:16). "We know that we have passed from death unto life, because we love the

brethren" (I John 3:14). Love for others is a desire for their salvation. If we are sold on the message of our Saviour, we will want to be salesmen for God. A salesman must be sold on his product, enthusiastic in his selling, and consider everyone he meets a prospect.

These are some of the results of having eternal life. These are the outward proofs of being in Christ.

Too well I remember sitting in a bamboo chapel in the Philippines and talking to the different people who dropped by to inquire about religion. During the day the most wealthy man of town stopped to chat. We gave special attention to answering his questions about America, business, and customs, etc. We talked for some time. Before he left, he was invited to attend our meetings. "Oh," he said, "I'm too busy to attend. Some day when I'm not busy I'll drop in."

It was a few days later that I was speaking in that chapel on the subject of "Winning Souls for Christ." The place was crowded, and as it was a hot day, the doors and windows were all open; the sound of a funeral band coming down the street came clearly to us. As the procession passed the church, I could see the faces of all who passed and hear the tramp of the many feet—the women singing their dirge, the children carrying candles; the priest holding the crucifix. Last of all, in the huge, carved black hearse, passed the man who had been too busy to attend our meetings. He was not too busy to die. But the thing that smote my heart that day was the fact that that man had been in the chapel just a few days before and I had not told him the way of salvation. I had let him go with a mere invitation to attend, nothing more. Now he was gone! I could not finish my message that morning. I had to stop and confess my sin before God. When I got right with God, then He worked in the church. That morning was the beginning of revival in the town. Others confessed their sin and were made right with God; even the leading men of the church and the pastor confessed sin; and for two hours that congregation was bathed in tears and repentance until every soul was right with God. Souls were saved. Re-

vival continued on for the two weeks of meetings that were being held. But it had to begin in my heart.

There are many prayers for revival these days. Christians and churches are praying and talking about revival. How can revival come? Just as soon as we are ready for revival! The price of revival is that we Christians get right with God and with each other, and then go out for God. Then we shall see revival.

God is ready to bless right now. The hindrance to revival is unconsecrated Christians with no burden for souls.

Are you a hindrance to revival? Am I?

QUESTIONS

1. What is eternal life? (John 14:6)
2. Why was the Gospel of John written? (John 20:31)
3. Can Satan separate us from Christ? (Rom. 8:35-39)
4. Who has eternal life? (John 3:36; I John 5:12)
5. Why was the Epistle of John written? (I John 5:13)
6. How long does everlasting life last? (John 10:28)
7. How do we get eternal life? (Rom. 6:23; John 1:12)
8. Who does the keeping of the Christian? (I Peter 1:5; II Tim. 1:12)
9. Do all who "profess" Christ really "possess" the Saviour? (Titus 1:16)
10. What is a backslider's interest? (Prov. 14:14)
11. Can a Christian sin and get away with it? (Gal. 6: 7; Rom. 6:2)
12. What are the five results of sin in the life of a Christian?
13. Do all Christians die because their work on earth is done? (I Cor. 11:30; I John 5:16)
14. What is the answer to soul hunger? (John 6:35)
15. What is the message of the Christian? (Phil. 2:16)

16. Can a Christian live in sin? (John 8:12; I John 3:9)
17. When we are a stumbling block whom do we sin against? (I Cor. 8:12)
18. Who seals the Christian? (Eph. 1:13, 14)
19. When are we saved? (Rom. 10:13; John 1:12)
20. When we sin, do we lose our eternal life? (John 5: 24; 6:47; Phil. 1:6)

11

RIGHTLY HANDLING THE WORD OF TRUTH

Study to show thyself approved unto God, a workman that needeth not to be ashamed, rightly dividing [handling] the word of truth (II Timothy 2:15).

ONE OF THE MOST COMMON COMPLAINTS of people today is, "I cannot understand the Bible! How can I ever know what it's talking about?"

We would all feel the same way, probably, if we tried to understand a book of medicine or science by reading hit-or-miss infrequently.

The Bible is a textbook on religion. It contains remedies for all our problems about salvation, the Christian life, harmony in the home, success in business, and even politics. Because it contains stories, that does not suggest that it should always be read from beginning to end. The best thing is to know where to find the special portions that will answer the particular need. After all, some books, some chapters are written especially for certain people, certain times, and certain needs. It is important to know which part of the Bible is for whom and about whom, which parts are especially for us, and which are especially for today.

It is amazing how the whole Bible fits into place like a giant puzzle when we know how to "rightly divide" or rightly handle the Word of truth.

There is no short cut to understanding the Bible, but

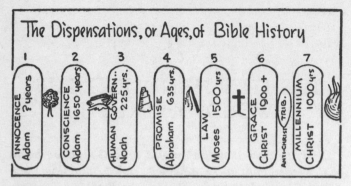

The Dispensations, or Ages, of Bible History

1 INNOCENCE Adam ? years
2 CONSCIENCE Adam 1650 years
3 HUMAN GOVERN... Noah 225 yrs.
4 PROMISE Abraham 635 yrs.
5 LAW Moses 1500 yrs
6 GRACE CHRIST 1900 + — ANTI-CHRIST TRIB.
7 MILLENNIUM CHRIST 1000 yrs

this lesson will help to give a key to the interpretation of the Word that might clear some of the confusion that even Christians seem to experience.

The Bible covers some thousands of years of man's history, past, present, and future, and in these years God has dealt with mankind in varied ways according to their understanding and the revelation from God, and according to the period of time.

These periods of time are called ages, or if you wish, dispensations. "That in the dispensation of the fullness of times" (Eph. 1:10). "Ye have heard of the dispensation of the grace of God" (Eph. 3:2).

The truth of salvation by faith in a Saviour has never changed throughout all history. Before the world was ever created, God had already planned for Christ to be "the Lamb of God who taketh away the sin of the world." "The Lamb slain from the foundation of the world" (Rev. 13:8).

To begin with, let us consider:

I. Prehistoric Time

This does not come under a dispensation since there was no man in the world. The original creation of the earth came "by the word of God" and out of nothing (II Peter 3:5, 6). It was a perfect world, perhaps a mineral and vegetation paradise with some animal life.

With the fall of Satan from Heaven, the "earth *became without form and void*" (Gen. 1:2), and chaos lasting for some billions of years would account for the coal, uranium, and other mineral deposits in the earth. There were periods of ice age, heat age and flood age. If there were prehistoric animals, they perished in this cataclysm (II Peter 3:6; Jer. 4:23-26; Isa. 24:1; 45:18).

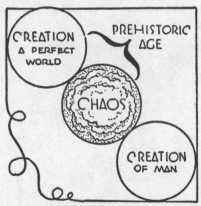

When God caused the earth to come forth out of chaos, as told in Genesis 1, He created man for the first time, and created animal life again. Each species was perfect in its own line, and God saw that it was good.

Mankind was created in the image of God (Gen. 1:27). This does not refer to God's physical image, for God is Spirit; it refers to the moral and spiritual image of God.

Adam and Eve were perfect mentally, morally, and spiritually, and also had a perfect physical body as well. Mankind did not evolve from any other species. Instead of *evolution*, it might be called *de-volution* or even better, *devil-lution*, because sin has degenerated man from his first perfect state and he has become weaker and shorter lived as the ages have passed.

II. The Seven Ages

A. THE AGE OF INNOCENCE— length of time unknown. How long Adam and Eve were in the Garden of Eden we do not know. When they chose to disobey God, they reaped the curse of God—Adam was to know toil and trouble and sweat; Eve was to suffer pain and sorrow and subjection to man; the serpent was to eat dust and travel upon its belly; all nature was to know thorns and blight and animosity (Gen. 3).

END OF THE AGE OF INNOCENCE

As each dispensation begins with God's blessing, so it ends with disaster as mankind disobeys God and reaps judgment. Adam and Eve were driven from the Garden of Eden.

B. THE AGE OF CONSCIENCE—approximately 1650 years. Now life begins outside of the Garden of Eden. God clothed Adam and Eve with the skins of animals, and so blood was shed as an object lesson of the blood of Christ who would be the Sin-bearer to take away the sin of the world.

Man's conscience now is his guide, and a very poor guide it is! Soon sin takes over again. Cain kills his brother Abel. Why? "Cain . . . was of that wicked one, and slew his brother. And wherefore slew he him? Because his own works were evil, and his brother's righteous" (I John 3:12). Cain's works were not acceptable because he did not bring a blood sacrifice for sin.

Man becomes worse and worse until God decided to wipe out the godless human race with a flood. For 120 years godly Noah preached the warning of coming judgment while he built the ark, but when disaster finally did come, only Noah and his family sought refuge in the ark of safety (Gen. 6-9).

C. THE AGE OF HUMAN GOVERNMENT—225 years. The ark is another type of the refuge we have in Christ from God's judgment. Now God begins the human race again with godly Noah and his family. From the three sons of Noah come the different races we have in the world today. Shem was the father of the yellow-skinned race; Japheth was the father of the white race; Ham was believed to be the father of the black race. It was at this

time that captial punishment and human government
were instigated by God (Gen. 9:3-6).

ΔGE OF HUMΔN GOVERNMENT

Once again, however, men turned away from God and
even thought to reach Heaven by building a tower that
would keep all peoples together and give them a name
on the earth. Men have always tried to find their own
way to Heaven and by-pass God's way of salvation. But
it does not work! This time God confuses their efforts
by confounding their languages so that none could understand the other, and the building had to cease. God
said: "Behold, the people is one, and they have all one
language. . . . Go to, let us go down, and there confound
their language, that they may not understand one another's speech. So the Lord scattered them abroad" (Gen.
11:6-8).

The very thing people had tried to avoid was now the
judgment God brought upon them. Men scattered
throughout the four quarters of the world. The age
ends in disaster.

D. THE AGE OF PROMISE—635 years. Once again God
begins with one man. This time, rejecting other nations,
God chooses Abraham and promises to make of him a

great nation. Through Abraham came the Saviour, "that the blessing of Abraham might come on the Gentiles through Jesus Christ; that we might receive the promise of the Spirit through faith" (Gal. 3:14) . "And the scripture, foreseeing that God would justify the heathen through faith, preached before the gospel unto Abraham, saying, In thee shall all nations be blessed" (Gal. 3:8; Gen. 12–50) .

Once again disaster hits, however, for the children of Abraham went down into Egypt where they became the slaves of Pharaoh. The age ends with the cry of the downtrodden, persecuted "chosen people."

E. THE AGE OF LAW—1500 years. Moses is the man God uses to liberate His people from Egypt, and give the commandments for their civic, religious, health and moral conduct. The law of Moses includes all the commands of the books of Exodus (including the Ten Commandments) , Leviticus, Numbers, and Deuteronomy, and any other commands that are found in the Old Testament. These commands were given to the Jews, and to them alone, until the Messiah, Christ, should come. "Wherefore the law was our schoolmaster to bring us unto Christ,

that we might be justified by faith. But after that faith is come, we are no longer under a schoolmaster" (Gal. 3: 24, 25).

The ordinances and rituals and sacrifices given to the Jews were all a type of Christ and His work of salvation.

This age of law ends with the greatest disaster of all time—the murder of the Messiah, the Son of God.

F. THE AGE OF GRACE: THE CHURCH AGE—1900+ years. This is the age in which we now live. Today God offers His salvation to "whosoever will," and not just to

the Jews. The "chosen people" today are those who choose Christ! As in the pre-Christ days, men looked by faith for the Saviour to come, so today we look back by faith to the Saviour who did come.

God deals with those who choose His way of salvation as His Church, His Bride, and His Body.

This Church Age or age of grace will end by the coming again of Christ to take His Church to be with Him and deliver it from the Great Tribulation that shall come. This tribulation is not a dispensation, but the disastrous ending of this age, and is an interlude of seven years called the Great Tribulation.

Because men have turned from God, disaster comes in the form of a world dictator, the Antichrist, who sets himself up as God and forces all mankind to worship him. Disaster in the heavens, chaos in the universe, and the whole of nature on the rampage are only paralleled by the bloodshed on earth.

G. THE KINGDOM AGE—1000 years. The tribulation ends with the coming of Christ to the earth to set up His kingdom in Jerusalem and the defeat of the Antichrist. The curse on the earth will be lifted and there will be

world peace, when all the world will worship the King of kings. This golden age is called the Millennium.

Even this Kingdom Age ends with the last revolt of Satan and the final disaster of the end of the world. "The heavens shall pass away with a great noise, and the elements shall melt with fervent heat, the earth also and the works that are therein shall be burned up . . . the heavens being on fire shall be dissolved" (II Peter 3:10, 12). (Scriptures on these last prophetic paragraphs will be found in the lesson on Coming Events in Prophecy.)

III. How To Interpret the Bible

With this general outline of the dispensations of Bible history, let us see how this can help with the interpretation of God's Word.

To begin with, except for the first eleven chapters of Genesis, most of the Old Testament is concerned with the history, laws, poetry, and prophecy of the chosen people, the Jews.

A. WE STUDY THE OLD TESTAMENT FOR INFORMATION. Its primary application is to, and for, the Jews.

The Old Testament is the Old Covenant, the old arrangement, that culminates in the sacrifice on Calvary.

The Old Testament was for the Jews, God's earthly people, and the primarily rewards for keeping the commandments were earthly prosperity, long life, large families, and living in the Promised Land.

The commands for the Jews are found mostly in the books of Moses, and include the Ten Commandments. Keeping God's commands could not take away sin; their failure to keep all the commands only showed men their need of a Saviour. "By the deeds of the law there shall no flesh be justified in his sight: for by the law is the knowledge of sin" (Rom. 3:20).

When men sinned in Old Testament days, they brought an offering of a lamb without spot and without blemish. But the blood of animals could never take away sin; it was a symbol that pointed by faith to the Saviour who should come. "For the law having a shadow of good things to come . . . can never with those sacrifices which they offered year by year continually make the comers thereunto perfect . . . for it is not possible that the blood of bulls and of goats should take away sins. . . . And every priest standeth daily ministering and offering oftentimes the same sacrifices, which can never take away sins" (Heb. 10:1, 4, 11).

Christ was a Jew. He kept the Mosaic law and rituals, and lived in the age of law. "God sent forth his Son, made of a woman, made under the law, to redeem them that were under the law" (Gal. 4:4, 5). Jesus kept the Jewish sabbath, the seventh day. His ministry was to "the lost sheep of the house of David." Many of His sayings and teachings were primarily applicable to the Jews and the Kingdom Age to come.

The Book of Matthew is especially to prove that Christ is the King of the Jews. The Book of Mark was written to the Romans to portray Christ as the Suffering Servant. The Book of Luke was directed to the Greeks, and shows Christ as the source of culture, the Great Physician, the Son of man. But the Gospel of John was written "that ye might believe that Jesus is the Christ, the Son of God; and that believing ye might have life through his name" (John 20:31). This Book of John might be called the peak of all the Bible, for although it tells of the life and words of Christ before His death, yet John recorded these events so very much later than most of the other New Testament books were written that the application is definitely for the Christian; it is in complete harmony with the writings of the apostle Paul and applies to our day since Christ's death.

B. WE STUDY THE NEW TESTAMENT FOR INSTRUCTION. This part of the Bible is directly *to* Christians and *for* Christians. Beginning with the Gospel of John, we have the Christian teaching of God's Word. There is no Christian before the death of Christ!

The dividing point of the Old and New Covenants is the death of Christ. Although the books of the Bible are divided at the birth of Christ, the change of teachings and application comes with His death.

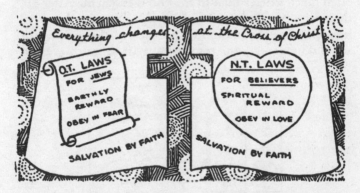

With the death of Christ the Old Testament was completed and fulfilled and laid aside, and the New Testament took its place. "He taketh away the first, that he may establish the second" (Heb. 10:9). The Mosaic law has been done away (Gal. 2:16; 3:11-13; 5:4, 18; Col. 2:16; Rom. 10:4; 6:6, 14; 7:6; 14:5, 6; II Cor. 3:7-11; Acts 15:24; 21:25). We are not told not to eat pork or keep the Jewish sabbath, etc.

Does this upset you? Are you throwing up your hands saying, "What! do Christians not even keep the Ten Commandments?"

C. STUDY OF THE TEN COMMANDMENTS. Look up Exodus 20 and read the Ten Commandments. To whom are they addressed? "I am the Lord thy God, which have brought thee out of the land of Egypt, out of the house of bondage." Have you ever been in bondage in Egypt? If not, then this is not addressed to you!

But does this mean that Christians may kill and steal and lie, etc.? Of course not!

Every command in the Old Testament that Christians are to observe is repeated in the New Testament!

Not only are the commands repeated, but they are often much stricter than in the Old Testament. After all, those who lived in the age of law did not have the privilege of having the indwelling presence of the Holy Spirit as we do today, so our responsibility is so much greater.

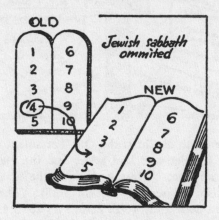

Then are the Ten Commandments repeated in the New Testament? Certainly; most of them are:

1. No other gods—I John 3:23.

2. No images (as aids to worship) —Acts 15:20; I John 5:21.
3. Swear not—James 5:12.
4. Remember the Sabbath—Christians are never commanded to keep the Jewish sabbath, the seventh day, Saturday. This is the only one of the Ten Commandments that is not repeated in the New Testament for Christians.
5. Honor parents—Ephesians 6:1.
6. Thou shalt not kill—I Peter 4:15.
7. Not commit adultery—Acts 15:20.
8. Not steal—Ephesians 4:28.
9. Not bear false witness, lie—Colossians 3:9.
10. Not covet—Ephesians 5:3.

Does this mean that Christians don't have to keep any day for God? Indeed not! It merely shows that we are not under the law of Moses to keep the day that was a special sign between God and Israel.

Then what day should we keep?

D. Why Do Christians Keep the First Day of the Week?

1. Christ rose from the dead on the first day of the week (John 20:1).
2. Christ met with His disciples after His resurrection on the first day of the week in the upper room, two different weeks after resurrection day (John 20:19, 26; Luke 24:13).
3. Pentecost came on the first day of the week (Acts 2:1).
4. The apostles met for preaching and taking of the Lord's Supper on the first day of the week (Acts 21:7).
5. The Christians were commanded to bring their offerings on the first day of the week (I Cor. 16:2).

The principle of keeping a rest day for God has

never changed, however. It is to be a special day, and not one that we walk through like every other day. "If thou turn away thy foot from the sabbath, from doing thy pleasure on my holy day; and call the sabbath a delight, the holy of the Lord, honorable; and shalt honor him, not doing thine own ways, nor finding thine own pleasure, nor speaking thine own words" (Isa. 58:13). The Christian's desire is to keep the Lord's Day in this same special way, a day of rest and worship, and not a day of outings, family reunions, housework, yard work, sports, etc., and neglecting the house of God!

The same principle in both!

E. WHAT IS THE SUMMARY OF THE OLD TESTAMENT COMMANDMENTS? When asked, "Master, which is the great commandment in the law?", Jesus answered, "Thou shalt love the Lord thy God with all thy heart, and with all thy soul, and with all thy mind. This is the first and great commandment. And the second is like unto it, Thou shalt love thy neighbor as thyself. On these two commandments hang all the law and the prophets" (Matt. 22:36-40).

F. WHAT IS THE SUMMARY OF THE NEW TESTAMENT COMMANDMENTS? "And this is his commandment, That we should believe on the name of his Son Jesus Christ, and love one another, as he gave us commandment" (I John 3:23). Notice how the principle of both the Old and the New are the same! The Old speaks of loving *the Lord thy God,* and the New speaks of loving *His Son Jesus Christ;* in other words, the Lord Jesus *is* God!

Now for just a moment, let us analyze the general commandments of the New Testament and see how they are to be obeyed to the glory of God *and* to show love for the souls of others.

LOVE GOD	LOVE OTHERS
1. Holy living (I Peter 1:14-16)	Righteousness toward man (I Thess. 3:12, 13)
2. Prayer (I Thess. 5:17)	Prayer for others (Eph. 6:18)
3. Bible Study (II Tim. 2:15)	To teach others (II Tim. 4:2)
4. Worship (Heb. 10:25)	An example to others (Matt. 5:16)
5. Witnessing (Matt. 10:32)	To win others (James 5:20)
6. Giving (Rom. 12:1-3)	That others might hear the truth (II Cor. 8:1-5)

You see, all we do in obedience to God is done for His glory to show our love to Him, *and* to show love to others that they might be saved. We cannot do any good works until we are saved. We are saved by faith in a Saviour. But when we are saved, we will want to obey God's commandments. The unbelievers came to Jesus to ask Him how they could please God. "Then said they unto him, What shall we do, that we might work the works of God? Jesus answered and said unto them, This is the work of God, that ye believe on him whom he hath sent" (John 6:28, 29).

We cannot do any works for God until we receive the Son of God as our Saviour. But if we have received Him, then our whole life is to live for Him and obey His commandments: "He that saith, I know him, and keepeth not his commandments, is a liar, and the truth is not in him" (I John 2:3-6). That's pretty straight language, is it not?

One of the stories not published in secular accounts of the sinking of the Titanic is the story of the preacher, John Harper. It was told by a pastor of a large church.

When the Titanic was sinking, one of those foundering in the ocean was a soul-winning preacher by the name of John Harper. Grasping a piece of floating wood, he pad-

HIS LAST CONVERT

dled around in the inky darkness from one sinking survivor to another asking, "Man, are you saved?" When the answer was, "No, I know my soul is lost!", he stopped long enough to explain the way of salvation and pray with the doomed man, and then paddled on to the next one. On and on during the dreadful hours after the great ship sank, John Harper swam from one to another with his message of salvation. And then, eventually, completely exhausted, and unable to hold on to his plank of wood, he himself sank beneath the dark icy waters.

That pastor who told the story closed his account with these words, "I was John Harper's last convert!"

So much stress is placed these days on the heroic efforts

to save human life; but human life will be short-lived at best, perhaps some one hundred years at the most, while the souls of men will live for eternity. How much greater the blessing of spiritual salvation that will save "a soul from death" (James 5:20).

Today the emphasis should be on spiritual miracles of the salvation of souls rather than the mere physical benefits of prolonging physical life.

There is a dear lady who loves the Lord with her whole heart, and everything she does is with the one purpose of trying to win others to love Him too. Of all heart-breaking home .conditions, however, she certainly had one of the greatest crosses to bear for her Lord, for her husband was not only antagonistic to religion but was brutal to her as well. Often she came to church with great bruises showing his brutality. But never was there a word of complaint. She had a radiant face and a radiant testimony.

For years she endured silently, and through it all the Lord blessed her witness to others with wonderful results She used to say to me, "I believe that God has allowed me to endure such testing so that I can better understand and help others." In truth, she literally loved others to God. Every act of kindness was linked with a word about salvation, every "cup of cold water" was accompanied with God's Word about the Saviour. She literally lived a life of obedience to God's commands, loving Him and loving souls.

It was some twenty years that she suffered in her home with that vicious husband. But then, things began to change. Bit by bit that man seemed to change. The last time I met them, he was kind, patient, and loving, and he told me his story. "I fought against God and my wife for twenty years," he said, "until I thought I'd go crazy with frustration and misery. Her sweetness and patience broke my heart at last, and I knew I wanted the Christ she so lived for each day. I too have found the Saviour, and what a joy our home is for both of us! But I do believe it was my wife's consistent living for God that eventually won me to Him. She is a saint on earth indeed!"

There is too much preaching and talking, and too little living for God these days! "What you are speaks so loudly I can't hear what you say!" is only too true!

God grant that when we know His commandments for us as Christians, we may obey.

QUESTIONS

1. Why should we divide the Scriptures? (II Tim. 2: 15)

2. What theme has never changed through eternity? (Rev. 13:8)

3. How do we know there was a chaos age? (Jer. 4:23-26; Isa. 24:1; 45:18)

4. What was the curse on sin? (Gen. 3:14-24)
5. Why did Cain kill Abel? (I John 3:12)
6. When was capital punishment given? (Gen. 9:5, 6)
7. Why was the law of Moses given? (Gal. 3:24, 25)
8. Could the sacrifice of the lamb take away sin? (Heb. 10:1-11)
9. In what dispensation did Jesus live? (Gal. 4:4, 5)
10. Why is the Book of John applicable for our day? (John 20:31)
11. Why don't Christians need to keep the Mosaic law? (Gal. 2:16; 3:11-13; 5:4, 18)
12. To whom were the Ten Commandments given? (Exod. 20:2)
13. Which of the Ten Commandments are repeated in the New Testament?
14. Why do Christians keep the Lord's Day, the first day of the week?
15. How should we keep the Lord's Day? (Isa. 58:13)
16. What is the summary of all the New Testament commandments for the Christian? (I John 3:23)
17. What is the first thing we must do to please God? (John 6:28, 29)
18. Does a Christian have to obey the commands of God? (I John 2:4)
19. What is more important than saving people's physical lives? (James 5:20)
20. Can keeping God's commandments save us? (Rom. 3:20)

12

COMING EVENTS IN PROPHECY

BEFORE JESUS CHRIST RETURNED to Heaven He promised, "I go to prepare a place for you, and if I go and prepare a place for you, I will come again, and receive you unto myself; that where I am, there ye may be also" (John 14:2, 3).

When Christ ascended into Heaven, a cloud received Him out of the sight of the disciples. Two angels said: "Ye men of Galilee, why stand ye gazing up into heaven? This same Jesus, which is taken up from you into heaven, shall so come in like manner as ye have seen him go into heaven" (Acts 1:11). Christ's return will be a bodily, literal return, not just a spiritual coming as when He comes into the hearts of persons who receive Him, or when He comes to take believers to Heaven when they die.

At His first coming as a babe in Bethlehem, He came to be the Saviour for the souls of sinners. But His second coming will be to save the bodies of believers when they will be resurrected to be like to His glorious body. Today Christ "ever liveth to make intercession for them" (Heb. 7:25). He is waiting until the last souls will be saved before He will return to the earth to take the believers to be with Him. To "love his appearing" means to hasten His return by trying to win souls so that He might return quickly. The second coming of Christ is in two events:

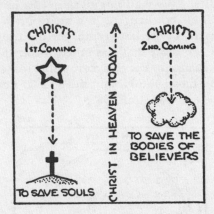

I. The Rapture (The first part of the second coming of Christ.)

We are now living in the age of grace, the Church Age, which began after the death of Christ and the coming of the Holy Spirit. This age will close with the first part of the coming again of Christ.

Just what will happen when He comes? No one will see Him. There will be no warnings. "For the Lord himself shall descend from heaven with a shout, with the voice of the archangel, and with the trump of God; and the dead in Christ [Christians' bodies] shall rise first: then we which are alive and remain [Christians who are still living on the earth] shall be caught up together with them in the clouds, to meet the Lord in the air: and so shall we ever be with the Lord" (I Thess. 4:16, 17).

The word *Rapture* is used to describe the "catching up" of the Christians to be with the Lord.

Notice, that the bodies of Christians who have died will be resurrected first, and then we who are still living on the earth will be caught up bodily to meet the Lord in the air, and our bodies will be changed into resurrection bodies. "We shall not all sleep [die in the Lord], but we shall all be changed, in a moment, in the twinkling of an eye, at the last trump: for the trumpet shall sound, and the dead shall be raised incorruptible, and we shall be changed. For this corruptible [physical body] must put on incorruption, and this mortal must put on immortality" (I Cor. 15:51-53).

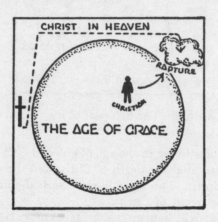

This is called "the first resurrection"; it is only for the bodies of believers. "Blessed and holy is he that hath part in the first resurrection: on such the second death [the lake of fire] hath no power, but they shall be priests of God and of Christ, and shall reign with him a thousand years" (Rev. 20:6).

Many ask the question, "Will we know our loved ones in Heaven?"

When we get to glory, "we shall be like him; for we shall see him as he is" (I John 3:2). We shall be like Christ morally, physically (with a spiritual body), and mentally. "For now we see through a glass darkly, but then face to face: now I know in part; but then shall I know even as also I am known" (I Cor. 13:12). Certainly we shall know each other in Heaven, just as Christ knows us!

Another question is, "Will we look like we do now?" One thing is sure, When we get to Heaven, we shall not measure beauty as man does now. God does not gauge beauty by the length of the nose or the bloom on the cheek or the proportions of the figure. Beauty is not skin deep with God! So when we become like Him, we shall measure appearance by His standards. To be like Him is wonderful enough for me!

Others wonder, "Will babies grow up in Heaven?" We know babies go to Heaven when they die, but as to whether they grow up or not we are not told. When the Bible does not tell us, then your guess is as good as mine!

Again, "How can a person be happy in Heaven if he knows his loved ones are in Hell?" When we get to Heaven we have the mind of God, and understand all things from His viewpoint. There will not be any problem when we realize why they are in Hell, for we shall think as God thinks.

Now, imagine the chaos and confusion that will ensue when suddenly the Christians are all caught away from the earth!

Automobiles driverless on the super highways will pile up traffic that will take days to unscramble; airplanes pilotless will crash where they will; machines without operators; operating rooms without surgeons; families without parents or children. And all in the twinkling of an eye! There will be no warning when the Rapture takes place. "Watch therefore; for ye know not what hour your Lord doth come."

It is important to remember that the Old Testament does not refer to the Church (except in type and occasional reference to the Gentiles who will turn to God). And so the final fulfillment of prophecies written before the death of Christ will especially be concerned with

Israel during the Tribulation and the Kingdom Age. Even the words of Jesus in the Gospels of Matthew and Luke regarding the "last days" primarily refer to the Jews who will pass into the time of "Jacob's trouble," the Great Tribulation. But this is also important to remember: "Coming events cast their shadow before." the closer we come to the end of this Church Age, there will no doubt be longer shadows of the beginnings of these preparations for the coming of the Antichrist. There will be movements toward unification of nations, labor and trade, and religions.

However, we *are* told to watch for certain signs of the times that will tell us that the Great Tribulation is near. "Now learn a parable of the fig tree; when his branch is yet tender, and putteth forth leaves, ye know that summer is nigh; so likewise ye, when ye shall see all these things, know that it is near, even at the doors" (Matt. 24:32, 33).

Just what signs did Jesus refer to in that passage?

A. THE SIGNS OF THE TIMES

1. *Israel*. The land that has for so long lain barren is to "blossom as the rose." The Jews are to be regathered

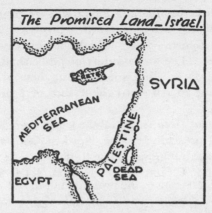

The Promised Land—Israel.

to their own land, and their government and language restored. All this has already been fulfilled. Israel is once again the garden country of the world with its irrigated groves and the return of normal rainfall. The wealth of the Dead Sea tempts all the other countries surrounding (Jer. 32:37, 43, 44; Deut. 28; Ezek. 36:34; 37:21; Joel 2:23).

2. *Wars.* But have there not always been wars? How do we know that *now* we are close to the coming of Christ? Yes, there have been wars, but never have there been *all* the prophecies coming true at the same time as they are now (Matt. 24:6, 7; Luke 21:9-11).

3. *Earthquakes.* Almost every day the newspapers tell of earthquakes. Never before in history have the scientists recorded so many quakes as in the last fifteen years. This prophecy has been fulfilled sufficiently (Matt. 24: 6, 7; Luke 21:11).

4. *World Conditions.* In preparation for the coming of the Antichrist, it appears there must be certain world alliances and situations. The "king of the north" (Russia) and the "king of the east" (the Orient) then will be in alliance. The "king of the north" and "Gomer" (Ger-

many) will be in alliance. Egypt will see trouble (Dan. 11; Ezek. 38).

5. *Peace Efforts.* There will be an increase of peace conferences. "The ambassadors of peace shall weep bitterly" (Isa. 33:7; I Thess. 5:3). But these peace efforts will continue to fail until the Prince of peace Himself shall come.

6. *Religious Decline.* In all the world there is a decline in truthful preaching of the Word of God, and an increase of false religions (Luke 19:8; Matt. 24:5, 11, 12; II Thess. 2:3; I Tim. 4:1, 2; II Tim. 4:1-4; 3:1-5, 13). This is now referring to the present church age.

Departing from the faith

This decline is called apostasy. Liberalism, or modernism as some call it is not up to date, but is as old as the Garden of Eden when Satan put doubts into the minds of Adam and Eve. Here are some of the main errors that are spreading in the main denominations today: All men are brothers and God is our Father; God is a God of love so all will get to Heaven some way; just keep the Golden Rule and do the best you can and all will be well; the miracles were just circumstantial happenings; Hell is here on earth, etc. Modernism or "Humanism" is trying to get to Heaven by man's own efforts. There are three stages,

and some churches are in the first, some in the second stage and some have gone as far as the third. The first stage is a worldly church, with dances and gambling, bazaars and raffles, etc. The second stage is a church where the message is weak and watered-down. It does not preach positive truth about sin and the new birth and the coming again of Christ. The third stage is blatant denial of the Word of God in denying the virgin birth of Christ, the miracles, the need for regeneration, etc.

7. *Travel and Knowledge.* Certainly as never before the earth is shrinking because of the increase of travel and communications and inventions (Dan. 12:4; Nah. 2:4). Within the last hundred years inventions have multiplied more than a hundredfold.

There is not yet one prophecy to be fulfilled before the return of Christ! He could come today!

When Christ returns, the day of grace will be over, and the opportunity for us who know Him to win souls will be ended!"

B. THE TRIBULATION PERIOD. Between the two events of the coming of Christ takes place the short seven-year-period of the Great Tribulation. "For then shall be great tribulation, such as was not since the beginning of the world to this time, no, nor ever shall be" (Matt. 24: 21, 22). After Christians are caught up to be with Christ, then Satan's Antichrist will be revealed on the earth. He

will be a miracle-man who can work miracles with the power of Satan. When he comes with flatteries and promises, the Jews will believe that he is their Messiah, and he will make a false peace on the earth for three and a half years (Dan. 11:21-24). Then he breaks his covenant with Israel and sets himself up as God; his false prophet forces men to worship him and the image he sets up. He takes over the whole world in political dictatorship, economic dictatorship, and religious dictatorship. He will be Satan's Christ (Matt. 24:15-26; Luke 21:25-28; Ezek. 38; Dan. 7:24, 25; 9:26, 27; 11:36-45; Rev. 13; II Thess. 2:3-12). He is called in Scripture the Antichrist, the Beast, the wicked king, the wicked, the son of perdition, the vile person, etc.

The tribulation will not only be caused by the workings of this incarnation of Satan who kills many who will not worship him, but the sun and moon and stars will be out of their courses, and the horrors mentioned in the Book of Revelation will come to pass. Remember that the woes mentioned in Revelation and poured out on the world will all take place in these short months of the last part of the tribulation. No true Christian today will experience them. Thank God!

There will be many who will turn to God during the tribulation days—"a great multitude, which no man could number, of all nations, and kindreds, and people, and tongues. . . . These are they which came out of great tribulation, and have washed their robes, and made them white in the blood of the Lamb" (Rev. 7:9, 14). Also there will be 144,000 from among the twelve tribes of Israel that will turn to God in those days (Rev. 7:1-8). It seems popular for some to claim that their followers are the 144,000! But these are Jews, and saved during the tribulation! And anyone who is of this number is unsaved today. He will be left behind when Christ comes and will be saved under the reign of the Antichrist!

So, many who turn to God during the tribulation will be killed by the Antichrist and his religious leader, the false prophet (Rev. 13:15; 20:4) because they will not worship the Beast or the image of the Beast.

Note this especially! Those who will be saved during the tribulation will be those who have not heard the

Gospel today! Those who have heard the truth today and rejected it, will not be saved. "They received not the love of the truth, that they might be saved. And for this cause God shall send them strong delusion, that they should believe a lie: that they all might be damned who believed not the truth, but had pleasure in unrighteousness" (II Thess. 2:10-12).

A man once said to me, "If what you say is true, and you suddenly are caught up and disappear, then I'll believe!"

I replied, "No, you will not! You have heard the Gospel today, but then you will believe the Antichrist and be damned with him!" That man is now a believer!

"And this gospel of the kingdom shall be preached in all the world for a witness unto all nations: and then shall the end come" (Matt. 24:14). The "end" is the end of the times of the Gentiles, and that will be when Christ comes to the earth to set up His kingdom, not when He comes in the air to rapture His saints. So it will be during the tribulation that there will be world revival, and the Jews will be the revivalists (Rev. 11).

What are the believers in Heaven doing during these seven years of trouble on the earth?

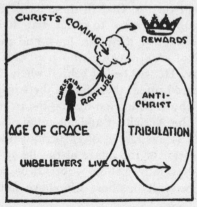

There will be the marriage supper of the Lamb, when Christ and His believers will fellowship together face to face (Rev. 19:7-9).

There will also be the judgment seat of Christ, when believers shall appear before Him to receive rewards or suffer loss. "For we must all appear before the judgment seat of Christ; that everyone may receive the things done in his body, according to that he hath done, whether it be good or bad" (II Cor. 5:10). This takes place in Heaven. It is not a judgment to see who goes to Heaven, but for rewards for our deeds.

"For other foundation can no man lay than that is laid, which is Jesus Christ." Christ is the foundation of our faith and of the church, and no one else is! "Now if any man build upon this foundation gold, silver, precious stones [obedience to the will of God], wood, hay, stubble [disobedience to God]: Every man's work shall be made manifest: for the day [the day of Christ, His coming] shall declare it, because it shall be revealed by fire [the testing of God. This fire is not purgatory, for believers are already in Heaven!]; and the fire shall try every man's work of what sort it is. If any man's work abide which he

hath built thereupon, he shall receive a reward [notice, he does not receive salvation for his works, but a *reward* after he gets to Heaven!]. If any man's work shall be burned, he shall suffer loss [it doesn't say that he shall be lost]: but he himself shall be saved; yet so as by fire [by the skin of his teeth!]. Know ye not that ye are the temple of God, and that the Spirit of God dwelleth in you?" (I Cor. 3:11-16).

What will it be when we stand in that day before our Lord? Will we hear His: "Well done, thou good and faithful servant . . . enter thou into the joy of thy lord," or will we "be ashamed before him at his coming"? (I John 2:28).

A Filipino lad was worried about what he would do with too many crowns, and asked, "Ma'am, how can I wear so many crowns at the same time?"

Knowing his hit-and-miss Christian life, I said, "Don't you worry about having too many crowns, Roberto, you've got a long way to go! But even if you do have many crowns, we shall not wear them and strut the golden streets. One of the thrills in Heaven will be to have something to cast at the feet of Him who loved us and gave Himself for us!" (Rev. 4:10, 11).

Anyway, "crowns" do not necessarily mean literal crowns, but rather rewards and approval. There will be four special joys in Heaven. First, face to face, we

shall see Him whom we love—Christ our Lord and Saviour! Second, we shall see others there whom we have won to Christ by our testimony! Third, we shall have a crown to give back to Him who gave it to us! And then we shall meet our loved ones who have gone on before us! Hallelujah!

A question is asked, "How can there be rewards in Heaven when everyone will be completely happy? How then can anyone suffer loss or be ashamed?"

Yes, we shall all be happy, but evidently there will be different capacities of happiness. Throughout eternity we shall remain in the degree of honor or blessing that we have earned, and there will be no chance to improve or make up for lost opportunities. Take a large bucket and a thimble, for example. Fill them both, and they are filled. But there is a difference of capacity! To enter into the "joy of thy lord" must mean a greater measure of enjoyment.

Christians will never pass through the tribulation "because thou hast kept the word of my patience, I also will keep thee from the hour of temptation [testing], which shall come upon all the world, to try them that dwell upon the earth" (Rev. 3:10).

Different Capacities!

II. The Revelation (The second part of the coming again of Christ.)

"Immediately after the tribulation of those days shall the sun be darkened, and the moon shall not give her light, and the stars shall fall from heaven, and the powers of the heavens shall be shaken: And then shall appear the sign of the Son of man in heaven: and then shall all the tribes of the earth mourn [the Jews will repent that they crucified Him], and they shall see the Son of man coming in the clouds of heaven with power and great glory" (Matt. 24:29-31; Luke 21:27, 28). "Behold, he cometh with clouds; and every eye shall see him, and they also which pierced him: and all kindreds of the earth

shall wail because of him" (Rev. 1:7). The wailing will mean repentance.

This takes place when the Antichrist will have gathered all nations against Jerusalem to battle (Joel 2:1-11; Zech. 14:1-5). This time the Lord comes with all His saints and every eye shall see Him. He is revealed as the Son of Righteousness with healing in His wings.

Christ will defeat the armies of Antichrist, and set up His own righteous kingdom, "the kingdom of God and of his Christ." This battle on the plains of Syria and

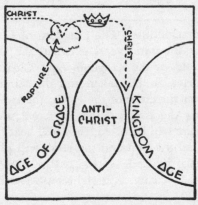

Palestine is called the Battle of Armageddon (Rev. 16:16; 19:11-21). The Antichrist and his false prophet are cast into the lake of fire, and their armies killed.

Then it is that all nations will be gathered before Christ, and He shall separate them as a shepherd separates the sheep from the goats. The sheep-nations are those which are kind to Israel, the national brethren of Christ, and the goat-nations are those which persecuted Israel (Matt. 25:31-46). The sheep-nations will enter the Kingdom Age of Christ to live on the earth with all those who did not participate in the forces of the Antichrist.

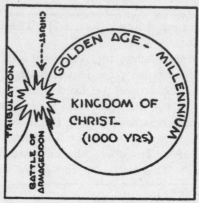

A. THE MILLENNIUM. The kingdom of Christ on the earth for one thousand years is called the Golden Age, the Millennium, or the Kingdom Age. Christ will make His headquarters in Jerusalem and the saints will reign with Him over the cities of the earth; the twelve apostles will rule over the twelve tribes of Israel; the curse on man and nature will be lifted; they will beat their swords into plows, and the lion and the lamb will play together (Isa. 2:1-5; 60:1-22; Zech. 14:16-21; Rev. 20:4-6). Success, plenty, health, security, and righteousness will reign supreme.

One reason for all this peace and light is that Satan is bound in the bottomless pit during the Millennium (Rev. 20:1-3). There will be no temptation.

B. THE LAST REVOLT. Strange as it may seem, even after the thousand years of Christ's reign, there will be men who will not love Him, and have only followed Him because there was no temptation. But now Satan is released from the bottomless pit and makes one last effort to gather men against God. He has good success too, for there is such a great number that they cannot be counted. One such is "Magog" or as we believe Russia (Rev. 20:7-10). But they do not get far in this revolt, for fire comes down from Heaven and devours them, and Satan is cast into the "lake of fire and brimstone . . . and shall be tormented day and night forever and ever."

C. THE JUDGMENT SEAT OF GOD—THE GREAT WHITE THRONE. Immediately after the Millennium, the unbelieving dead are resurrected for judgment. This is called the second resurrection (Rev. 20:11-15).

All who come to this judgment are cast into the lake of fire. They come before God merely to receive the degree or sentence of punishment. All who stand before the Great White Throne are already condemned, they do not get a second chance. There is no second chance after death (Rev. 21:8). A special place of punishment is reserved for those who teach wrong doctrine (Jude 12, 13).

Thank God, no Christian will ever stand before this judgment seat of God! He promises those who receive Christ as their Saviour that they "shall not come into condemnation; but is [are] passed from death unto life" (John 5:24).

No, we shall never stand before that last judgment throne, but we shall be there to watch. As the unsaved stand there to be cast into the lake of fire, will some neighbor or friend of yours, some relative or loved one, stand there and point at you, and say, "You never told me!"

God says: "When I say unto the wicked, Thou shalt surely die; and thou givest him not warning, nor speakest to warn the wicked from his wicked way, to save his life; the same wicked man shall die in his iniquity; but his blood will I require at thine hand" (Ezek. 3:18, 19).

Christians, are we guilty? Do we have the blood of the lost on our hands?

D. THE WORLD DESTROYED. The end of the world does not come for over a thousand years after the Rapture, but when it comes the heavens and earth will be dissolved into gases from which God makes a new Heaven and new earth. "The day of God, wherein the heavens being on fire shall be dissolved, and the elements shall melt with fervent heat. Nevertheless we, according to his promise, look for new heavens and a new earth, wherein dwelleth righteousness" (II Peter 3:12, 13).

Perhaps someone will ask, "But why all this about coming events? Who cares what comes in the future? To live for today is sufficient." Well, the Word of God tells us: "Seeing then that all these things shall be dissolved, what manner of persons ought ye to be in all holy conversation [living] and godliness, looking for and hasting unto the coming of the day of God. . . . Wherefore, beloved, seeing that ye look for such things, be diligent that ye may be found of him in peace, without spot, and blameless" (II Peter 11-12, 14).

The new heavens will be a new universe (not the Heaven of God), and it will be on the new earth that all perfected and resurrected saints will be with Christ forever in bliss and have access to the Holy City and the Heaven of heavens.

It is vitally important how we live today because our eternity depends upon it. Sometimes we hold these temporal things on this earth so dear, and forget that "the world passeth away, and the lust thereof; but he that doeth the will of God abideth forever" (I John 2:17).

When Christ comes it will mean that Christians have no further opportunity to win others to God. The opportunity to win rewards is over, the joy of glorifying Christ before the unsaved is gone. Our day of serving our Lord is now, in this day of grace. Just what are we doing about it?

When God chose Saul to be king of Israel and they went to find him to crown him king, they could not find him. He had hidden himself among the baggage! Perhaps he was afraid of the responsibility, or timid of the publicity, or shrank from the heavy burden of work that being king might involve, but whatever it was, his excuse was not good enough to allow him to shirk the call of God to serve. He was found.

Christ has called each of us Christians to win souls. What excuse do we have for shirking His call? His eye can see through any excuse. He can see us hiding among the "baggage" of our excuses, and pretty poor excuses they are too!

While very ill recently, I spent one night close to death. I was alone in the house and experienced one attack after another when my heart threatened to stop beating and the pain seared my chest and arm. As each attack came on I expected it to be the last, and I remember so well praying, "Lord, take me home to Heaven now. I'm homesick for Heaven." As I recovered consciousness again, I was vaguely disappointed to find I was still in this sad old world!

Then as I lay and waited for the next attack to come, I began to think of the many souls around me that I had not yet reached with the Gospel. I thought of those in my Bible classes whom I had not yet dealt with regarding their salvation. I thought of the many who were new in the faith and had recently accepted Christ. I thought of the many meetings scheduled ahead when unsaved people would be coming to listen to the Word of God. My prayer changed. I found myself praying for those souls, praying that if God wanted me to serve Him a little longer that I might do my very best in the time remaining.

Oh, Christians, why is it that we so often have to face the valley of the shadow of death before we realize afresh the need of the world around us! We think we are ready to see Christ, but just what have we done for Him? Are we really *ready* to die? Have we done our best for Him? Will there be many in glory because we have been faithful in our soul-winning? Will we have to stand empty handed before Him at the judgment seat of Christ?

Unsaved friend, what will it be for you when Christ comes again? Will you be left behind? You have now heard the way of salvation, and you will have no excuse before God at all. Will you be left to go through the Great Tribulation and to believe the Antichrist? Will you stand before the Great White Throne of God and be cast into the lake of fire? Is this what you want?

Why not right now say, "Lord, I know I am a sinner and that Christ is the only Saviour. Please come into my heart right now and save me, save me from the tribulation, from the judgment, from Hell, and from sin."

Just recently I was asked to visit a woman in a hospital. When I first visited her she was very independent and self-righteous, and asserted, "I'm no sinner! I've never killed anyone!"

"That's strange," I said, "for God says you are a sinner even though you haven't killed anyone."

We read the Scripture about all being sinners, and showed the way of salvation and how to be born again; as we talked she became more and more concerned. That day before I left she prayed and asked Christ to save her.

I visited her a few more times, but I could see she was failing fast. I was glad that during that first visit she had been able to listen and understand God's Word. Three weeks later I came into her room to find that she had been taken only half an hour before. Her bed was empty, she had departed this life. How glad I was that I had heeded the call to visit her, and that she had seen her need of the Saviour before she was ushered into eternity!

Too often other calls have come to visit the sick, and they have been too ill to listen, and some had already died. So often people wait until they are sick or some calamity comes before they give real thought to eternity. Why offer to God a dying life when He wants our whole life in health to serve Him? No one would offer to their loved one a bouquet of wilted flowers, yet men and women offer themselves to God when they are too ill or too old to serve Him!

Yes, the future is coming, whether we look ahead or not.

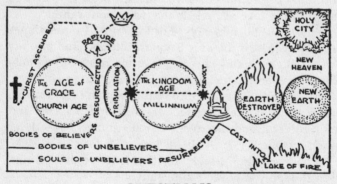

QUESTIONS

1. Is Christ's coming again a literal bodily return? (Acts 1:11)

2. Where do we get the word *Rapture*? (I Thess. 4:16, 17)

3. When do living Christians receive their resurrection bodies? (I Cor. 15:53)

4. Who takes part in the first resurrection? (Rev. 20:6)

5. Will we know each other in Heaven? (I Cor. 13:12)

6. When will Christ return? (Matt. 24:42, 44)

7. What are the signs of the times?

8. What happens between the two parts of the coming of Christ? (Matt. 24:21, 22)

9. What does the Antichrist do to those who will not worship him? (Rev. 13:15)

10. How many Jews will be saved during the tribulation? (Rev. 7:1-8) .

11. Who will not be saved during the tribulation? (II Thess. 2:10-12)

12. Who comes before the judgment seat of Christ? (I Cor. 3:11-16)

13. When does Christ come to set up His kingdom? (Matt. 24:29)

14. Will Israel ever receive Christ as their Messiah? (Matt. 24:31; Rev. 1:7)

15. What is the judgment of the Antichrist?   (Rev. 20: 7-15)

16. What is the judgment of the sheep and goats? (Matt. 25:31-46)

17. How long will Christ reign on the earth? (Rev. 20: 4-6)

18. When is the second resurrection? (Rev. 20:11-15)

19. Will Christians be judged at the last judgment? (John 5:24)

20. What importance do the coming events have for us as Christians? (II Peter 3:11)

Moody Press, a ministry of the Moody Bible Institute, is designed for education, evangelization and edification. If we may assist you in knowing more about Christ and the Christian life, please write us without obligation to: Moody Press, c/o MLM, Chicago, Illinois 60610.